YOUR HAPPILY EVER AFTER

Your Happily Ever After Honouring Your Most Sacred Relationship; The One You Have with Yourself © Lauren Jobson, first published 2023.

Lauren Jobson asserts the moral right to be identified as the author of Your Happily Ever After Honouring Your Most Sacred Relationship; The One You Have with Yourself

©Intuitive Heart Publishing

All rights reserved. No part of this publication may be reproduced, stored in a retrieval system or transmitted in any form or by any means, mechanical, electronic, photocopying, recording or otherwise, without the prior written permission of the author.

This book and any associated materials, suggestions and advice are intended to give general information only. The author expressly disclaims all liability to any person arising directly or indirectly from the use of, or for any errors or omissions in this book. The adoption and application of the information in this book is at the readers' discretion and is his or her sole responsibility.

Your Happily Ever After Honouring Your Most Sacred Relationship; The One You Have with Yourself

National Library of Australia Cataloguing-in-Publication entry:

Jobson, Lauren, 1986 -

ISBN: 978-0-646-86295-8

Edited by: Karen Crombie at Exact Editing.

Author and cover photograph: Zahrina Robertson.

YOUR HAPPILY EVER AFTER

Honouring Your Most Sacred Relationship; The One You Have with Yourself.

LAUREN JOBSON

Contents

Foreword by Pip McKay
3

Introduction
7

MIND
Chapter 1 - I Vow to Understand My Mind in A Loving and Compassionate Way.
I honour the relationship I have with myself.
17

BODY
Chapter 2 - I Vow to Love My Body.
I honour the relationship I have with the home I get to live in and experience life through.
47

HEART
Chapter 3 - I Vow to Live in Alignment with My Highest Values.
I honour the relationship I have with my heart's priorities.
79

POWER
Chapter 4 - I Vow to Make Self-Loving Decisions.
I honour the relationship I have with my power.
103

SELF-TALK
Chapter 5 - I Vow to Talk to Myself with Perspective, Compassion & Forgiveness.
I honour the relationship I have with my judgements and inner voice.
135

EMOTIONS

Chapter 6 - I Vow to Listen to and Respect My Emotions.
I honour the relationship I have with my feelings.

161

SPIRIT

Chapter 7 - I Vow to Honour My Own Path and to Trust in The Big Picture of My Life.
I honour the relationship I have with a higher connection to myself.

193

CONNECTION

Chapter 8 - I Vow to Take Ownership in My Relationships.
I honour the relationships I have with self-loving boundaries and communication.

227

PHYSICAL WORLD

Chapter 9 - I Vow to Take Action with Supportive and Intentional Behaviours.
I honour the relationship I have with my external world and how I show up in it.

257

Final thoughts to my reader
288

A note from my grandmothers on self-love
289

Lauren's gratitude
290

About the Author
295

References
297

Connect with the Author
299

Dania Zafar School of Hope
300

Dedication

I dedicate this book to my grandmothers; Nan and Abuela and to my mum and mum-in-law, who paved the way.
To my sisters, my daughters Amber and Aurora, and my niece Hazel.
To my nephews Jake and Lachlan.
Self-love is a process for everyone.
This book is particularly dedicated to all daughters in this world learning to love ourselves amongst it all.

Thank you to my husband, Brendon.
Thank you for showing me myself and
being a mirror for my growth.
Thank you for allowing me to grow my
light in the light of our love.
This book and a lot of my progress through my career simply wouldn't be what it is without your love and support. This book literally wouldn't have been birthed if not for you being the domestic King you are, putting on the washing, cooking, and cleaning most days to allow me to escape into my office.
Everyone deserves the generosity of understanding, love and support that you give to me.
Thank you, my love.

Foreword

Have you ever wondered why people struggle with self-love? After all, the relationship we have with ourselves is the most intimate and impactful connection we can ever have. Yet many people adore their pet more than they like themselves. They would never speak to an acquaintance the way they berate themselves. They would never mistreat even a stranger the way they neglect themselves.

Why do we do that to ourselves and how can we change it? That is what *Your Happily Ever After* by Lauren Jobson is all about and why it is such an important contribution to our world.

Many people don't realise that how we love ourselves impacts the quality of all our relationships. Those who really love us, fundamentally want us to be happy. Self-love is the corner stone of that well-being. So, we make our loved ones very sad when they witness us hurting ourselves, even if it is only in our mind. When they can't do anything to help us, we make them feel powerless. Many people believe they are hiding their treatment of themselves, but this is delusional. Those close to us pick up on our mood, even if only unconsciously and it becomes an example of how they too should treat themselves.

It is a tremendous show of love to others, to love ourselves.

It makes them feel happy to be around someone who is joyful, confident and has self-esteem. It is also a shining example for others to follow. As a result, changing the way we treat ourselves and having resources to enhance self-love is essential for us, our families and our communities. It helps make the world a better, healthier environment for all.

With that in mind, I was very excited when Lauren asked me to write the foreword for her book. In its pages, Lauren beautifully shares the vulnerability and strength of her own experiences. She then guides us to discover our own answers to essential questions such as: Why do we sometimes fall short in self-love? How can we heal? What can we do to love ourselves more effectively in the future?

By reading this book you will go deep into your heart and connect with your soul. Through it, Lauren acts as your personal coach, supporting you with her exquisite humanity, wisdom and love. She shines a light to illuminate your path back to yourself.

I first met Lauren in 2010 when she came to my home for an intimate, invitation-only evening about archetypes. When she walked through the door, I immediately knew there was something special about her. She had a curiosity, intelligence and understanding that belied her years. It came as no surprise to me to discover that she was Australia's youngest ever NLP Trainer and was already running her own business as a sought-after coach and trainer.

She also loved my work and ended up doing all the Evolve Now! Courses I created. She then became an Archetypal Coaching® Trainer and Matrix Therapies® Master Trainer. In fact, I was so impressed by her, she became my very first licensee of those programs and one of only two Master Trainers of Matrix Therapies®.

She has gone on to transform thousands of people's lives with her very special message of self-love and transformation. Now with her book, *Your Happily Ever After,* she will be able to reach thousands more.

In this book you will soon discover that Lauren has a unique ability to reach out of these pages to engage your heart and touch your very soul. So, you too can transform your life, love yourself more deeply and be a guiding light for others to follow.

Thank you, Lauren, for being you! You are such an exquisitely beautiful human being with a spirit that lights up the world. I am so blessed to call you my dear friend.

With warmth,
Pip McKay
CEO of Evolve Now!
Amazon Number 1 Award-Winning Author
Creator of Matrix Therapies® and Archetypal Coaching®

Introduction

Travelling home from my college job at eighteen, I remember sitting on a train reading a book and feeling so deeply connected to the author's writing and what she was saying about human potential. I felt compelled to stand up in the train carriage and tell everyone to read a book because it could change their life! It was a vivid moment in my memory because it was one seed of my soul's calling coming through in my life. My passion for knowing we have more potential and depth than most realise had been ignited.

It was not my first experience with this calling, as you will read in Chapter One. Still, it seems significant to mention here because I realised how much a book could speak to us and make us feel deeply understood and seen.

This book you hold in your hands has been within me for over a decade and took a couple of years to write, capturing the meaning and essence of my message to you.

If I had written this book last year or next week, I would be different and have a slight variation of perspective as I thought about the chapter concepts. Sure, the basic theory would be the same, but writing is a creative process, and just like anything creative, it asks for life energy to bring it into being, and the wise words of my parents ring in my ears, "You can't control anything that is living but yourself." I found myself adding and changing many words to this book after the birth of my second daughter, which has informed another level of my writing and changed my world again. And so, if my writing happened in divine timing for me to capture these particular words on these pages, then I firmly believe that you, my beloved reader, are also reading this in perfect timing.

This book being a long time coming is one example in my life of how having self-belief in our dreams and taking persistent action to fulfil our heart's desires can be a process. Overcoming our self-doubt, developing our confidence and courage and growing in our capacity to fulfil our potential sure is a process. This is just one message that will come through quickly in this book: we all fear and have doubts and inner criticism, yet it is up to us what we do going forward which makes all the difference in our lives. I want to inspire and show you how to step more into your capacity for love, growth, happiness, and success, whatever success means to you.

I am so honoured and excited to share this book with you, bringing clarity to the ambiguous topic of self-love. A concept that is varied in understanding and is such a personal topic when it comes to the experience and perception of what it truly means.

Who am I to teach Self-Love, and why learn about it from me?

My answer to this question is quite simple compared to the topic itself. While, I don't have more confidence or self-belief than the next person and I have struggled to find my place in the world as many people do, I have a healthy relationship with self-love. I always come back home to myself and persist in pursuing what my heart calls me to. In each chapter of this book I'll share a different example of coming home to myself through my personal stories, and reveal for you a new layer in finding self-love.

Even as I write this to you, I have been experiencing a higher level of discovering who I am and working through self-doubt and self-imposed limitations. I have been continuing to ask myself how I can live more of my potential, with life asking me to believe in myself more than ever. Life is not always easy – in fact, when is it ever? - I feel life is fundamentally about growing into who we want to become.

We are not born confident. We choose confidence. We are not born loving ourselves because we do not even have a concept of being separate from our mother. Generally, when we are little, we mostly have experiences where we can innately love who we are. Still, sadly, the reality is, for most human beings, life itself here on earth has us creating all sorts of mixed-up meanings of how we feel about ourselves and what it means to be *us* in this big wide world.

One of the motivations to write this book has come from my experiences teaching personal development training courses since 2009 and having the privilege of certifying thousands of students across Australia and now internationally, thanks to online training. I have learned it is in deeply understanding not just **who** we are but **how** we are the way we are that truly helps us.

It serves us as human beings to know how to unravel the places in our past that still lead us into pain so we can then weave our true essence into the lives we want to create for ourselves. In acknowledging the places of pain or growth, we can understand how we came to where we are, so we are then able to create a relationship with ourselves which is truly unconditionally loving. Hence, 'Your Happily Ever After' (only one of the two reasons for this title; you will discover the more important reason in Chapter One).

When we are self-loving, we understand how to create the feelings, experiences, behaviours, and outcomes that feel the best to us, are best for us and the best for the greater good for all.

To me, self-love is all about how we return home to ourselves. It is how we act, reflect, learn, and then let go if we need to forgive ourselves for something. Life is not perfect; we are beautifully imperfect, so we need to realistically allow ourselves **to be all of who we are** and to strive to be better when we need to. Self-love is the underlying way we come back home to ourselves when we feel we have gone off our path, by comparison, self-criticism, or by behaviours which are not aligned with our heart's highest priorities. Self-love is a process and a sacred relationship with ourselves. It is the most important relationship in our lives. Treasure it. Treasure you!

I've had the idea on my vision board for almost a decade to write a book titled: *Life Lessons for Our Daughters*. Because even before I was blessed with biological daughters, I knew one of my most important purposes in life was to share the message to all women (and men, of course!) of just how much we can (and should) love ourselves unconditionally. I see this for the greater benefit of all humanity, for each of us to be more of who we really are; by disconnecting from the patterns of the old, which no longer serve us or the world today, whilst respecting and holding on to the great wisdom of our elders.

In doing this for ourselves, we do this for all future generations, and we effect evolution itself due to the way we have lived.

To sum up the content of this book, these five concepts define self-love to me: process, forgiveness, relationship, honour and devotion.

Self-love is Process

Self-love is not something you either have or don't have. Instead, it is a journey and a process of growth. We are all in that process at every moment of every day. I will talk a lot in this book about ways to come back home to yourself and deepen your relationship with who you are. One of the best ways to do this is to understand and acknowledge that being human means going out into the world to learn. In the process of learning, we will have polarities of experiences. In between it all, we choose to put meaning to them, which dictates how we place ourselves in the world according to what we go through and creating the way we see ourselves. This is all part of that process. Life is a process and when we fully realise this, we can forgive if we need to and tell ourselves, "I'm just in process."

Life is forever moving, which means we can't ever be truly stuck but can take the next opportunity to be in the process of learning and growth.

Self-love is Forgiveness

To be in the process of learning and growth, we really need to practise self-forgiveness. We need to be forgiving ourselves continually. For the things we wanted to do and didn't. For the things we felt we could have done better, but we didn't.

Finding ourselves in certain situations we shouldn't have been in, but were. For behaving, reacting, or interacting with another human being in a way that was not the most loving. We need to forgive ourselves for it all. Love can't shine through as wholly as it needs to when there is a block in the energy that is guilt, shame, regret, anger, resentment, or any other emotion that depletes our happiness.

To forgive is to listen to the lesson, take the learning on board and move forward. All of us have things we wish we had done better and perhaps had times we cringe over when we think of how we behaved. We all have these times, and we will very likely have more. Live, learn and be gentle with yourself. You are a human moving through the learning experience that is life, and since we all have times and places where self-forgiveness is needed, we might as well choose to do whatever it takes inside of us and in action outwards to allow ourselves to move on completely.

Self-love is Relationship

One definition of a relationship is "the way in which two or more people or things are connected or the state of being connected." I believe self-love is a relationship between all parts of oneself. To me, self-love is the relationship we have with:

- ♥ how we understand our own mind and respect how it works for us,
- ♥ the connection we have to our bodies, which is fundamentally the vehicle which carries our spirit/soul through this physical, human existence and is our only home to live and experience life through,

- ♥ knowing our values, which are the most important priorities in our lives, and which motivate our hearts to be happy and fulfilled,
- ♥ making self-loving decisions to continually discern what is no longer best versus what we want to have more of in our lives, whilst creating beautiful boundaries,
- ♥ paying attention to how we talk to ourselves, which is the way we make judgements and what, in turn, contributes to our behaviours and the energy we express in who we are being,
- ♥ listening, acknowledging, and understanding our emotions so we can respect them for the loving messengers they are, invitations for us to grow,
- ♥ a bigger picture for our life and feeling connected to something higher than ourselves, feeling supported and guided with a meaning for our lives,
- ♥ our relationships with others and the loving communication and personal power we show up to others with, and
- ♥ appreciating our environment with how it supports us to create a life we love through the actions we take, with self-loving and intentional behaviours.

Self-love is Honour

The Oxford Languages dictionary definition of honour is "to have high respect" and "great esteem", "the quality of doing what is morally right", and "to fulfil an agreement". One description I particularly love when it comes to defining self-love is "a quality of a person with social teaching of high ethos, expressing a code of conduct with integrity, honesty and compassion."

This is why each chapter in this book explores one of the nine relationships I mentioned above through learning a vow we can have to honour ourselves. I will teach certain concepts that make these vows possible for us to keep. Each a sacred promise to ourselves.

It is in having a healthy relationship with all parts of us and in all areas of our lives. When we can honour ourselves and these relationships, we grow our self-awareness to experience more success on our terms.

Self-love is Devotion

The Oxford Languages dictionary definition of devotion is "love, loyalty or enthusiasm for a person or activity". I love this because, in the context of self-love, it's 'love, loyalty and enthusiasm for self and also for the activity of learning to love oneself'. As mentioned above, self-love requires the acceptance of it being a process – an active process of devotion. We must be so devoted we forever choose to come back home to who we are and who we want to be, to choose to show up for ourselves.

Devotion asks us to commit, particularly in areas of our life where we have half-heartedness. For many people, there is half-heartedness when focusing on self. We are rarely shown how to commit deeply to self; instead, it's expected we focus primarily on others and respond to the outside world with all of its influence. It is time to appreciate how our mindset up to today, our personality, and how we experience life has been shaped through our experiences and the perceptions and meaning we attach to them.

How to get the most out of this book

I wrote this book in the order I intended it to be read. I start each chapter sharing a different part of my life in order to build a relationship with you, my beloved reader, and to allow my story to be an example, illustrating the topic of each chapter.

You may see some correlations in my ideas with such things as the chakras, Gestalt Therapy, psychology principles and even ancient wisdom such as the Hermetic Eastern Mystery Tradition, which includes Astrology and Archetypes, plus Human Design and Gene Keys. It is important to me that credit is given where credit is due for all wisdom which has come before me, so I will reference my sources throughout the book and at the back of the book. This book and the ideas you will read are a culmination of my creativity and expression of my learnings. This book is a pouring out of my heart, and I hope you feel the love and tenderness in my words.

I have created a workbook with all the activities I mention in each chapter, and you can access it at: www.laurenjobson.com/bookfreecourse

Let's get started together right now.

All my love and faith in your potential,
Lauren
Master Trainer, Transformational Therapist & Coach in NLP, Matrix Therapies® and Archetypal Coaching®.
www.laurenjobson.com/bookfreecourse

Chapter One

I Vow to Understand My Mind in a Loving and Compassionate Way.

*I honour the relationship
I have with myself.*

Vow One

> *"Patients are patients because they are out of rapport with their own unconscious... Patients are people who have had too much programming - so much outside programming that they have lost touch with their inner selves."*
>
> MILTON H. ERICKSON – HYPNOTHERAPIST.

The day I understood how my mind worked changed my life forever. The sensations of deep sadness I had been repressing until that moment of understanding, rattled my body with pure emotion. After many years of terrible pains in my stomach, which caused me to be crippled with feelings of hopelessness, there was one question that changed the course of everything.

It was in the middle of a school day, I must have been able to miss a class as I was in my uniform, and mum dropped me off to see my therapist for another session. It was warm, and I was feeling curious, filled with much anticipation to discover what we would talk about this time. I quite liked the mysterious nature of the waiting room and my therapist herself. It was an old, rundown building, upstairs from some shops on the side of the Pacific Highway which is a busy main road that goes all the way up the edge of the state of New South Wales in Australia. The waiting room at the top of the steep staircase was dark, yet intriguingly inviting. I looked up at the intricacies of the ceiling the old building had. Wondering what stories the ceiling was telling with all the history it held.

At the tender age of sixteen, I was known as "the girl with the tummy aches." I don't know if you have ever been identified by your problems? Or know someone whose self-identity is so closely bound with an illness or past painful experience? It is all-consuming. It affected every area of my life. I was sick during our family holidays and going out with friends on the weekend. I was ill at school, home, and everywhere else – it was soul-crushing. I thought so much about wanting to be better, yet my body was not getting the message. It kept feeling a dull ache that would ebb and flow in intensity. I would be curled over in turmoil, feeling a sense of hopelessness that life would never feel any better.

My parents had taken me to many different doctors, including psychologists. I'd taken every physical test they could think of to find out what caused this very real pain. I had nights in hospital and many times of utter despair where my parents, friends and family had no idea how they could help me. No answers had been found. We all felt we would just have to find ways to cope with this part of who I was. I wished with every cell of my body to no longer have this part make up who I was. I felt willing to do whatever it took to be different; I just didn't know how.

One night, I was at a concert with my uncle, a huge inspiration in my life. After having a dance to Jamiroquai, I started to get the all-too-familiar pain and felt terribly sick. My body expelled all joy from me again, both literally and emotionally. That night my Uncle Simon saw me suffering and realised just how much he wanted to help. He felt compelled to recommend the woman who would become my therapist.

On this particular day, she invited me into a much brighter client room. It smelt warm and nurturing from the oils she must have rubbed onto her skin. Her soothing voice instantly made me feel safe and comfortable. This time I sat in a reclining chair instead of the usual one. She guided me through a beautiful visualisation of being in a safe place in my mind's eye. Before I knew it, I deeply, deeply relaxed.

All I could do was trust my imagination. It was easy to continue following her suggestions. By the time she asked this one vital question, I could instantly connect to the deeper knowing part of me that just allowed my thoughts and feelings to be.

'Lauren, if you were to name the cause of this round, black thing in your stomach, what would it be?'

The answer came through me from somewhere deep inside; something was powerfully bubbling up that I hadn't consciously thought of before. The vibration of this emotion came up from my stomach, through my throat and out my mouth before I could even judge it. In a torrent of tears, I blurted out:

'Because my biological father didn't love me. I'm not worthy of being happy and healthy,' whilst an image popped into my head of me as a toddler, playing in the park and feeling this way. I saw myself, as a little girl experiencing my father's absence. I felt it was all my fault and I wasn't good enough for him to stick around.

During this session, I connected with my inner child, and was able to let her know I indeed loved her, her biological father is just one man, and she would grow up to be me, who was safe, loved, cherished and adored – even if it was just me who felt these things for her now. I am blessed to be loved by the people in my life as a bonus. How could she *not* be loved by me; this innocent little girl who is perfect in every way?

I went back to school afterwards and remembered sitting in my English class, feeling my whole world had changed. That evening I had a huge cry and felt the familiar pain in my stomach show up. I, finally, could consciously acknowledge what had been hidden deep inside my unconscious mind. I realised how I had questioned my place in the world and what it meant to be me, because I did not know the love of my biological father. It was to be a final purge of this pain.

After that day, I never had a stomach ache again.

This was twenty years ago. It was only the beginning of my awakening into personal development and self-love. The beginning of my passionate journey into the potential we all have to make deep, lasting and profound change.

The catalyst of this change can be the power of our inner wisdom; the power of the connection we can have with our unconscious mind. The part of our mind where all our memories are stored, where our emotions and behaviours come from. Where all meaning of ourselves takes shape. It is the part of our mind that is intimately connected to our body and how it functions.

Our relationship with our mind

The first relationship we need to fundamentally understand

is the one we have with our incredible mind.

I wish we were told as young people we are not our thoughts. We would live incredible lives and create more success if we knew not to take our thoughts so seriously! If only we were educated about our minds! It's important to know; how do we form thoughts? Why do we think specific thoughts? How can we identify what is a helpful thought which can contribute to a healthy relationship with who we are and what we want to create in our lives, and what is not? We'll explore why we tend to default to negative thoughts in Chapter Six but for now, let's see how they are created in the first place.

Our conscious mind and its limitations

In the personal development or human potential field, it is well known our conscious mind is only a tiny percentage of our mind's capacity. Most people don't understand the voice inside their head and what they are focussing on at any given moment, is such a small part of them. Compared to the rest of their mind's potential, which sits in the unconscious mind.

Professor Snyder at the Centre for the Mind, University of Sydney, who studied savants (very talented people) and mind science, said in an interview with Pip McKay in 2001, that our conscious mind is only four percent of our mind's capacity. He also said if we were to expand this to just six percent, we would all be geniuses. This is incredible for us to understand because it shows how powerful we are and what we are aware of in any given moment is just a tiny aspect of our potential.

Our conscious mind is like a torch shining the light into

our inner wisdom, which resides in our unconscious mind. For example, think of your phone number now.

Before you read the above question, where was your phone number sitting in your mind? Were you constantly repeating the numbers in your conscious awareness while reading this book? No, you were not. Instead, your number was residing in your unconscious mind. The moment you read the sentence asking you to think of it, you had the torch of awareness shining the light into your unconscious mind as you searched for your phone number. When you have your number in your awareness, it's now in your conscious mind.

Our focus determines what we shine the light on. What we focus on with our attention – our conscious mind – is what we are asking our unconscious mind to bring up for us. What happens when our external environment asks us to think of something more complex than our mobile number? Is it our conscious mind that determines how we react to our external environment, because it is only around four percent of our mind's capacity? No, our unconscious mind indeed informs what we focus on and the meaning we put to it. Our environment influences what we are asked to shine the light on every moment.

From my story in this chapter, it was the external environment created by my hypnotherapist which asked me to shine a light on the cause of my stomach pains. It was not my conscious mind answering this question. It came straight from my unconscious mind. I didn't walk around knowing the limiting belief I had made about myself. It was my little girl inside me, who felt the absence of her biological father and created the meaning from it she wasn't good enough or loved. My body then functioned from this place because our unconscious mind also runs our body which I'll explain more about soon.

This is also why willpower doesn't work when we want to make any changes in our lives. Getting rid of a habit for example or starting a new behaviour like exercising can't suddenly be generated by thinking about it if we don't engage the deeper parts of our mind at the same time. We usually need to make a change in what we value and our beliefs around the topic too (we explore these in Chapter 3). We may also need to change our perception of a memory like I did with my perception of myself regarding not knowing my biological father. In the final chapter in Chapter Nine, we learn how to change our behaviours or start new ones. This is what I love about NLP as it explains how we behave and why.

Now is the perfect time to dive into the less discussed but more influential part of our minds – the unconscious mind.

Our unconscious mind and what it does for us

Our unconscious mind is the part of our mind where all the non-conscious information sits. We could call it the subconscious, the not-conscious, or perhaps the unaware mind. It works differently to the conscious mind, which is the part of your mind running the thoughts you are aware of in each present moment. There can be other terms and official labels for different parts of the mind such as some people will say there is both an unconscious mind and subconscious mind. The point to make though is this is all metaphorical because we have one mind and we are simply labelling the different functions of how it works for us.

Our amazing unconscious mind is where all our emotions come from, our memories are stored, and where all our behaviour's function, hence it's where real change occurs. Our unconscious mind looks after our body, so we don't ever have to think about beating our heart, blinking our eyes, digesting our food, regenerating every cell, and so on. It does so much for us!

Our unconscious mind creates and determines what we focus on. It is the part of us directing our awareness and what we shine the light on. It is where our feelings are created, where our visualisations inside our minds are formed from and also how we talk to ourselves. Yes, it is our unconscious mind which determines our self-talk, too. This is how we work as human beings. Let's now look at the interaction between our unconscious and conscious mind by a model we love in Neuro Linguistic Programming (NLP) which is a sophisticated set of personal development and communication tools.

I love the NLP Communication Model because it shows the paradox of human beings in that we are such different and complex beings, yet we all work the same way. This model simplifies human behaviour whilst including and honouring the complexity of how unique and different we all are.

The NLP Communication Model

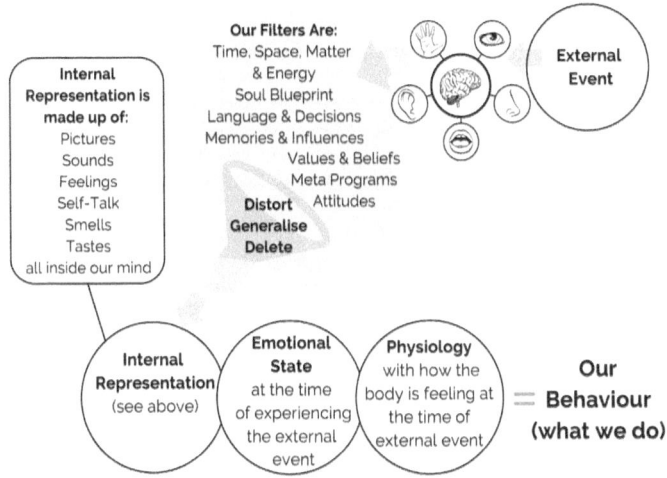

The NLP Communication Model in the diagram above is a foundation for understanding the universal question of why we do what we do as human beings. Instead of asking why in NLP, we focus on how. When we can understand how we create our behaviours, it answers the question of why, too. With how, we can have a process to work with as we can break it down into the steps we take to produce specific outcomes – our behaviours. This model beautifully describes how we do what we do as human beings by outlining the steps both our thoughts and actions take to get the results we have in life.

We start at the model's top right hand side by receiving an external event through our five senses. Inside the head, you can see next, we distort, generalise and delete the external event, depending on our internal filters. Our filters include time, space, matter and energy (the environment we are in), our soul's blueprint (this is my addition to the model outside of NLP which includes the idea we are born with information to work with – explained by our human design, astrological birth chart, our soul's chosen archetypes etc – we go over in Chapter Seven), the language we speak and the words we use both to ourselves and others. Additionally, our decisions, memories & influences which make up our experiences and what we make meaning from, personality types (called meta programs), values, beliefs and attitudes. All of these filters determine how we process the external world and create perception and meaning.

Distorting, generalising, and deleting information is a quick, unconscious process we all need to do. We simply cannot cope with the unbelievable amount of information that is said to be bombarding our senses every second of our day. We are habitual beings because we are a product of our environment. How we filter all the information from outside of us informs how we respond and act according to our perceptions internally. We create our perceptions and create meaning to events based entirely on the filtered information.

An analogy to understand this model is how we use filters for water purification. Just like we run tap water into a jug which holds a filter, and once the water runs through it, we are left with cleaner water to pour into a glass for a drink, so too are we left with specific results once we have filtered our external world. Our behaviours are the clean water.

Here is an example. Two people are watching the same movie, and one person laughs at a particular scene whilst the other person may be moved to cry in empathy for the character. Two people are having a different experience and reacting to the movie because the information of this external event has gone through each of their own filters of their memories, values, beliefs etc. In turn, they have created a different internal representation with unique meanings as to what the onscreen character is experiencing. One person may laugh because they have had the same problem as the character in the past but have solved it for themselves or they simply can't relate to it. The other person may be crying because they are going through the same pain in their life at the time of watching it.

More specifically, imagine the show is about a character who falls pregnant accidentally and it's intended to be comical about the idea of questioning who the father is -think Bridget Jones "The Edge of Reason", is a movie about exactly this. Now someone who hasn't experienced any trauma around fertility could find this movie funny. Yet for someone else, like myself, having experienced significant pain in getting pregnant would be experiencing this movie completely differently. Particularly if watching it while going through the journey of wanting to get pregnant and deeply struggling.

What are distortions?

Distortions are helpful for our imagination and goal setting to make our reality what we would like it to be. Distortion means changing the details of an event that is happening outside of us or the way we think about an event inside our minds from how they really are. Examples of distortions are all the ways we tell ourselves stories and different meanings to things that either serve us or don't. They are our criticisms, judgements, perceptions, and even excuses we come up with. A simple example is distorting a memory such as thinking our friend wore a blue shirt yesterday when it was purple. It can also be when we mishear someone's communication by distorting it in our mind to fit our perception of what we think they said. We've all had times when we continue a conversation with someone, and it becomes a misunderstanding because our perception has distorted what the other person meant versus the meaning we have created.

What are generalisations?
Generalisations are helpful, so we do not need to relearn basic things repeatedly. An everyday example might be seeing every different chair we come across and generalising it to be a piece of furniture we sit on. They are the basis of stereotypes and assumptions that if one thing occurred as it once did, then that same thing would always be that way. For instance, one could generalise the belief all relationships are hard work due to being hurt in the past by an ex-partner. This is an all-too-familiar generalisation affecting how someone can perceive potential new partners and dismiss them altogether because of the filter of past hurtful memories. We can of course generalise in any area of our life such as thinking all exercise is not pleasurable for example, when really, a generalised belief like this stops the person from finding a type of exercise they love to do and can persist with.

In fact, all limiting beliefs have been formed from our generalisations. My limiting belief about not being good enough as a person was a generalisation from one experience of my biological father not being in my life. It is when we take a significant, emotional event and generalise it to apply to a greater context. Such as, a child may not think they are good at catching a ball after a small amount of disheartening experiences. They may generalise this to believe they are not good at sport. From experience with a ball generalised to not being good at all sport is now a self-limiting belief. Again, all limiting beliefs are generalisations. They stop us from seeing different options and possibilities.

What are deletions?
Deletions are helpful to process the most meaningful information in our conscious mind and then delete the rest of it, so our awareness is not overloaded. Deletions remove specific information from our awareness that is right there in front of us, in our environment. When a person is feeling extremely negative, they have completely deleted all the positive things in their life at that moment. A more trivial example would be when we have had glasses perched on our heads or are holding our keys and still wonder where they are as we look around for them.

Common deletions we make in everyday communication occur when a person has an entire internal representation of what they are talking about in their minds but only share a small amount of detail with their words and expect the other person to fill in the detail accurately. An internal representation is when we play a movie of a memory in our mind, we have a feeling and know exactly what we are talking about, yet we delete parts of what we are thinking with the words we use to the other person. For example, using words like "we", "they" and "he" can be misunderstood easily because certain information is not specified as to who we are thinking about.

Or when someone says, "oh yes, the idea we had is such a great idea" and expecting the other person to know what idea they were referring to from a conversation days ago. The communicator has deleted the information of explaining what idea they are referring to simply because they can picture it all in their mind and forget in the moment the other person is not thinking of the same picture at the same time.

Communication is always key to recover distortions, generalisations and deletions that we all make every day.

All these filters (time/space/matter/energy, our soul blueprint, the language we think and speak in, decisions, memories, our influences on us, values, beliefs, meta programs, and attitudes) and then what we delete, distort, and generalise according to these filters, are unconscious. For example, we do not need to have a memory pop into our conscious awareness before the external event emotionally triggers us. Our body responds as a sensation like a fast heartbeat, a drop in our stomach, a tightness in our chest, all before we are consciously aware of why. Since our body is where all our emotions, memories, and behaviours come from, we start behaving from any unresolved emotional place inside our unconscious mind right away.

It is when we become aware of all our unconscious programming and have an understanding of;

- ♥ why we feel the way we do,
- ♥ why we have certain self-talk, and
- ♥ why we behave the way we do,

that we can make a change if we want to. Create our lives

the way we want to, and live with intention, passion, growth, and meaningful contribution.

I am so passionate about this topic I have it as the first chapter of this book. It is also one reason for the book's title, because "Your Happily Ever After" refers to the marriage we have within ourselves. It is when the masculine and feminine nature inside each of us are connected and we can give birth to a new version of our potential. We can learn to love ourselves unconditionally. Let me introduce this concept to you now.

The relationship to our sacred marriage within

Let's think about our mind as an ideal marriage. We want our conscious mind to connect to our unconscious mind so we can live intentionally rather than in a reactionary way (as mentioned earlier).

If something is sacred, it is of high importance and deserving of respect. The definition of marriage is the legally or formally recognised union of two people as equal partners in a personal relationship. Our relationship with ourselves is of high importance, it deserves respect, and is a vital union between our conscious and unconscious mind.

When I speak of this sacred marriage within, it is about the interconnection between masculine and feminine energy and how beautifully they can flourish when they work together and support one another. Please note, I am in no way, shape or form suggesting that marriage is between feminine and masculine persons only, because I am talking about energies. These energies go beyond any gender. I want to make it clear I believe in marriage between any individuals and am simply honouring the feminine and masculine nature we all have, every single person having their unique mix of these two energies.

Each energy comes with different resources which we will go over next. For thousands of years, the conscious mind has been represented as a masculine concept and the unconscious mind as a feminine concept.

Our conscious mind is masculine

Masculine energy is the conscious part of us. This energy we speak of has nothing to do with gender, yet we can use what we know of the male reproductive organs to understand it. The penis and testicles are outside of the body, producing an outcome of sperm and ejaculation. Compared to the female reproductive organs, which are hidden and internal. Anything we can label clearly and is something we can easily make sense of and see outside of us, is masculine in nature. Anything which is hidden and can't easily be labelled or seen, is feminine in nature. Every time we breathe out, we are in our masculine energy and every time we breathe in, we are in our feminine energy.

When we are aware of what we are reading, we are in our masculine energy. When we go inside our minds, influenced by what we have read, and conjure up pictures and internal connections to what we have read, we go into our feminine energy. Whenever we ask ourselves a question, we are being masculine, and searching for the answer inside of us is feminine. So, the conscious part of our minds is masculine as it is aware and projects form. Here are some other times in our lives when we are tapping into our masculine energy:

- Breathing out
- Taking action
- Speaking
- Goal setting
- Focussing on the external world
- Organising
- Planning
- Getting results and achieving our goals.

The very nature of something popping into our awareness at any given moment means it has form, a boundary with which we can label it and hence is our incredible masculine energy.

Now, let me take this to a deeper level for you.

Suppose we have a problem with any of these things above, such as:

- discipline,
- organising our lives,
- knowing what we want through goal setting,
- focus and concentration, or
- taking action

we can assume there is some unresolved energy to do with a masculine role and influence in our lives. Generally, this is represented by a father figure, and if we have any issues such as abandonment feelings, trauma from this person, or simply not experiencing the fathering we wanted as a child. This can manifest into problems with our masculine energy; hence, we stop tapping into the resources of the masculine such as not being able to organise or discipline ourselves. To resolve this, working with a therapist or coach trained in Matrix Therapies® will help. As a result, we learn to father ourselves. I will talk about how we do this soon.

Our unconscious mind is feminine

Feminine energy is the unconscious mind. As you go inside your mind to make internal pictures of what you are reading and connect this information to yourself to understand this, you are being feminine. When we listen and are open to receiving the answers to our own and others' questions, we are in our feminine energy. Here are some other times in our lives when we are tapping into our feminine energy:

- Breathing in
- Being still for inner reflection
- Listening to someone speak
- Meditating and journaling as you receive what you want to write
- Focussing on our inner world – imagination, thoughts, emotions and how our body feels
- Receiving
- Being in our body by feeling the sensations and emotions as they are
- Giving birth to our creativity by using our imagination wisely.

If we go deeper with this concept:

Suppose we have a problem with any of these things above, such as:

- ♥ The ability to receive anything we want in our lives, even the ability to receive compliments from others,
- ♥ being still and truly relaxing,
- ♥ exploring our inner world of thoughts, emotions, and beliefs,
- ♥ using our imagination wisely and
- ♥ giving unconditional love to ourselves

we can assume there is some unresolved energy to do with a feminine role and influence in our lives. Generally, this stems from a mother figure, and if we have any issues such as abandonment feelings, trauma from this person, or simply not experiencing the mothering we wanted as a child, these can manifest into problems with our feminine energy. To resolve this, working with a therapist trained in Matrix Therapies® will help. As a result, we learn to mother ourselves. We will explore this soon.

Another important aspect of understanding our sacred marriage within is to understand from this marriage, we want to give birth to our newly regenerated, best selves. Our thoughts and actions fertilise our emotions and imagination. This means we need to be our own ideal mother and father.

We all grow up physically and appear as adults. Yet, unless we go within and are willing to parent ourselves, we will continue to look to others for approval, love and acceptance, which only keeps the results we want to experience in our lives away from us. Our physical parents were there for us to be able to grow and learn about the adult and human being we want to become.

We need to do the work inside ourselves to resolve the gap between the innate expectations we had for how we wanted to be parented and our actual experience of it. Babies are born expecting unconditional love, nurturing, boundaries to keep them safe, adoration and attention, the list goes on. Human beings innately know what to expect from parents. Regardless of what we think and how we feel now as an adult about how we were parented, growing up, there were many times we made meaning to the outside world and how we fit into it that no longer serve us. For as long as we hold negative energy from our pasts, we stay stuck in our emotional and mental bodies, taking us away from our power in the present moment.

I discuss more about our emotional bodies and our power in the following chapters.

A lot of us don't consciously think we have unresolved stuff around how we were parented but what does affect us unconsciously are all the things we learnt from them about the world and what meaning we made about ourselves growing up. Even if we feel we had wonderful parenting because it's very possible we did, our inner child will always have experienced things and adopted beliefs, emotions and behaviours from our parents that do not serve us now as adults – simply because we are separate and unique human beings living in a different environment to what our parents did. I go over this in great depth in Chapter Four with how this is not about blaming our parents. Rather, it is resolving the negative perceptions we have made about ourselves due to our past experiences.

It is worth becoming conscious of anything we would like to let go of that we picked up from our parents for any area of our life. Do we want to manage money like our parents did? Do we want to do health the way they did? Do we want to have the same beliefs about what it means to have a job? The list goes on.

This is not about blaming them and entirely about turning the focus on healing ourselves to take responsibility for the results we want in our lives and create who we want to be from our own choices rather than from old unconscious programming.

Fathering ourselves through our masculine energy

When we talk about our masculine nature, we are, more specifically and importantly, talking about fathering ourselves. To father ourselves means to apply all the positive resources of masculine energy in our lives. If I were to have you understand just one idea of how to be your own father, it would be this:

We need to create structures which allow for our unique potential to flourish. This means being able to have insight into how we work best in terms of the following:

- what motivates and inspires us?
- what tools and systems could we use which are aligned with our unique energy?
- how do we work best when we let go of external expectations?
- what do we want to achieve in our lives?
- what actions do we need to take to accomplish our goals?

To have insight into all these things above means we can create structures to help us be more of who we are. The more we can be ideal fathers to ourselves, the more we can grow up and mature our emotional, mental, and spiritual selves.

What do I mean by structures? Think about anything that helps you live and show up in your daily life to be functional and productive. It is how you discipline and organise yourself and use external tools and systems to complete tasks. Examples of this are the routines and rituals which end up becoming habitual. You might even forget they are a routine or habit. It is the steps to look after yourself and any dependants, such as what you do each morning to start your day and how you then organise your to-do list throughout the day.

To be your ideal father, you must make sure you are creating systems and only using tools that work best for you and how you function. If getting up at 5 am, only to be exhausted for the rest of the day where you don't get anything done occurs, then expecting yourself to join "The 5 am Club" (yes, it is actually a thing) and have it work out is not realistic. In this instance, having this insight could have you understand that you work better by getting your sleep in the morning and being discerning about any advice on when you should be getting up. Your masculine energy wants what works for you, whatever allows your potential to flourish.

Mothering ourselves through our feminine energy
When we talk about our feminine nature, we are, more specifically and importantly, talking about mothering ourselves. To mother ourselves means to apply all the positive resources of feminine energy in our lives. If I were to have you understand just one idea of how to be your own mother, it would be this:

We need to love ourselves unconditionally and always come back to having compassion and understanding of ourselves. Perhaps this entire book could be seen to help us do just this. Being our own mother could be the most crucial role for us to play when it comes to our self-love. To be able to mother ourselves, we need to make sure we have enough compassion and willingness to understand ourselves. Underneath all this, be open to the fact we are all innately loved and worthy. We need to unconditionally love ourselves enough to know this. I want this book to at least introduce the possible opportunities and tools you might need to become your ideal mother and father. This is one of the most significant concepts I help my clients and students understand and experience.

Other ways we mother ourselves include:

- Being vulnerable enough to open ourselves up to receive what we want and to be able to do this we need to - Nurture ourselves enough to resolve our inner wounds, address limiting beliefs and resolve negative emotions which still sit in our bodies and unconscious mind.
- Finding creative ways to solve problems and to use our imagination in a self-loving way.
- Learning to just be, instead of always pushing for results and output that is not aligned with who we are and what is truly right for us.
- Respecting and working alongside the acceptance of cycles – from the cycles of life to seasonal cycles, down to any personal monthly cycles if you menstruate.
- Listening to and following our intuition.

Conclusion of this vow

I vow to understand my mind in a loving and compassionate way.
I honour the relationship I have with myself.

Our inner children crave to be seen by our present selves and to be given the resources they felt they missed out on while growing up. If we don't connect to these unresolved parts of us, we will continue to look outside of ourselves thinking that perhaps competing with others, having more material things or recognition will somehow have us feel loved, accepted and safe. It is always up to us to parent ourselves by tapping into the resources of both masculine and feminine energies.

We can give our inner children everything they ever desired because all they ever wanted is to fundamentally be seen and understood, to be loved, feel worthy and to feel safe with self-acceptance. Many people don't ever learn to do this, so they literally stay stuck as children walking around in adult bodies. We all have childlike behaviours, and we are continually learning to grow ourselves up and come back home to ourselves with unconditional love and acceptance. I go over this in *Archetypal Stages of Growth* by Pip McKay in Chapter Four.

The most self-loving thing you can do is to connect more deeply with yourself by listening and paying attention to what is going on for you inside your mind. Checking in with your emotions and not repressing them with coping mechanisms but instead truly listening to what the emotion wants you to learn. In Chapter Six I will be covering how to do this.

This is your sacred marriage within. It is the honouring of living in an external world (masculine) and always taking personal responsibility for your inner world (feminine) too. Sometimes it takes just a few more resources to know how to do this for yourself so you can feel you are the creator of your own life. Learning to become our own best parent is self-loving.

Our sacred marriage is our happily ever after, not because

we will be happy in every moment of our lives. Instead, we can find true unconditional love for ourselves because we have a path back home. When we are connected to ourselves and are willing to do what it takes to deepen this connection, we will always return to our innate happiness and peace.

    I want this for you. I hope you want it for yourself, too, and if there is part of you that feels uncomfortable in wanting to receive this completely, keep reading! This book can also give you the resources to let you know you are worthy of this happiness and are more than enough to give it to yourself. You wouldn't deny a child you love these things, so it's time to see yourself for the divine child you have always been.

A summary of what you learned in
Chapter One

I Vow to Understand My Mind in a
Loving and Compassionate Way.

I honour the relationship I have with myself.

- Lauren's story on how letting go of her limiting belief healed her stomach pains
- Our relationship with our mind
- Our conscious mind and its limitations
- Our unconscious mind and what it does for us
- The relationship to our sacred marriage within
- Our conscious mind is masculine
- Our unconscious mind is feminine
- Fathering ourselves through our masculine energy
- Mothering ourselves through our feminine energy

Devoting yourself to applying the learnings in this chapter:

1. Using the Self-Loving Resources of Tools and Mindset: Grab your journal or use the free course I created for you at www.laurenjobson.com/bookfreecourse where you can answer the below questions and more, online.

Ask yourself the powerful questions below and any others you want to add, including those asked in the fathering ourselves section with what motivates and inspires you etc. Go within to listen to what answers come to you and write them down without judgement or questioning. No one else needs to see your answers, so go ahead and deepen your connection to your unconscious mind by practising the act of simply listening and acknowledging your wisdom within.

Q1. What does self-love mean to me?

Q2. How healthy do I feel my level of self-love is right now? What number would I give it out of ten and why?

Q3. What beliefs do I have about what it means to love myself?

Q4. The positive things I love about myself are…? Write down at least ten things!

The rest of this book will elaborate on how to make sense of why we do what we do and how to take action to improve our lives and to grow ourselves up.

2. Using the Self-Loving Resource of Support: A Matrix Therapies® and NLP Master Practitioner can help you change the patterns in your unconscious mind and the meanings you have created about life and yourself that no longer work for you. This will also allow you to let go of any negative influences in both masculine and feminine energies so you can learn to be your ideal parent. Matrix Therapies® is also wonderful for the practise of forgiveness.

3. Using the Self-Loving Resource of Action: All of the information in this chapter could just be interesting theory until we devote ourselves to taking applied action. Answer the questions above and be sure to grab your journal and use the tool of my online course.

4. Using the Self-Loving Resource of Forgiveness: This is a reminder that life and self-love is a process. Do what you feel drawn to and practise forgiveness. Particularly self-forgiveness. I also like EFT (emotional freedom technique) for forgiveness as the script is beautiful: "Even though I (state problem), I deeply and completely, love and accept myself". I will share resources on how to do this in my online course. Again, doing Matrix Therapies® is also wonderful for the practise of forgiveness.

Chapter Two

I Vow to Love My Body.

I honour the relationship I have with the home I get to live and experience life through.

*"You're not your body, you're not your mind,
you're so much more, you've been here before.
You're a sweet spirit soul, more precious than gold.
Full of treasures untold."*

SONYA FURLONG'S SONG, "SWEET SPIRIT SOUL".

I have seven half-siblings. It doesn't feel right to define it like that because I have siblings I am very close to; there is nothing half about them. And biologically, it is true. I am one of six children from my biological father, who he had with four different women. One of those is my amazing mum. She had been working in the UK for a while and was making a life for herself, far away from where she grew up in Australia. Then she met this seemingly charming man.

Before I was born, my mum cared for this man's two oldest children as her own. He also had another child before me, with another woman. That would be the beginning, it seems, for a pattern of him procreating and quickly moving on, disregarding the children he was so blessed to have made.

His fourth child was me, after being with my mother for a while. My sisters were eight and seven when I was born, they adored me and loved having a baby to look after like their own.

We were a happy family for a while. We had a house, two dogs, a mum, a dad and three of us girls. Of course, I do not remember this because I was just a baby. I was always told these things growing up and was shown photos of the big family trip we took to Australia on holiday to see my Mum's parents and the family. We looked like a happy family, going to the theme parks and my sisters having fun on the rides with my aunt and uncle (my mother's siblings) and swimming and sitting in the spa; all those fun things families usually do on holiday.

These happy family times were not to last, and once back in the sweet home they had made in the UK, the cracks of his character began to be revealed more and more to Mum.

One day, Mum suspected my father had just been with another woman. This time she was going to say something to him. I was six months old at the time.

"Are you having an affair?" she asked him, straight out.

He wasn't used to being questioned, confronted or held accountable. This sparked one of his usual outbursts of rage. When he saw Mum reach out for the phone to call the neighbours for help and comfort, he pulled the phone line so hard out from the wall that the entire phone flew across the room, part of it hitting my face whilst I was snuggled in Mum's arms.

He saw that he had hurt me and might have felt a little bit bad about that, so he didn't stick around to see the consequences of his actions. Instead, he walked out of the house. That was the end of him living with us. That was the end of him being my father in any way. Neither of us ever spoke to or saw him again.

Unfortunately, my mum had no legal custody of my two older half-sisters. I was to learn, very sadly, that my mum and I needed to say goodbye to them and leave them in the loving care of their grandparents. They were so young when the woman they regarded as a mother figure and their baby sister had to leave for the other side of the world. I can only imagine how we all felt at that confusing and emotionally intense time. I was too young to remember it consciously yet part of me had always remembered this great loss. Like some parts of me would be missing.

This story has a happy ending I will share in the opening of Chapter Nine, but for now, I want to show here in this chapter how the circumstances we are born into can inform so much of how we experience life. The events of how I entered and began my childhood affected my body in the form of chronic stomach aches as a teenager and resulted in a significant turning point for me with how I overcame them. Let's explore the relationship we have to our bodies and just how special it is in storing our experiences for us and more.

Our relationship to our body - Body image is ours for the making

I want to start with this point because many of us can get stuck identifying ourselves with how we look. What we look like is just a perception, which can be so twisted and far from the truth; it's a shame we can be so attached to body image. We can destroy a lot of self-love from the idea we are what our bodies look like. The good news is we can create how we feel about our bodies, which can entirely shift our experience of life and our relationship with our bodies. Consequently, the amount of joy and gratitude we can reclaim.

Body image is yours for the making. You get to decide what labels you use for your body and what meaning you put to the information your body is simply providing. Talking from personal experience, it didn't change my happiness level when I put on 20kgs over five years and also lost 10kgs in a shorter time. It changed my energy level and vibrancy, which created more confidence. Since there are many other ways to gain energy and confidence, regardless of weight, we can choose for our weight to be redundant with regards to how we feel about ourselves. This is not always easy to do in a world where many influences tell us how much weight is important. It is not. You don't love people in your life any less or more with how they look, so why do we treat ourselves with less love? We get to decide.

Our perception of how others perceive us creates confidence. We either think positively about how we express ourselves to others, or not. We can change our confidence level at any time by changing how we feel about ourselves. If we think and feel others think we look unattractive, we will feel unattractive, regardless of what others are actually thinking.

When our bodies change over the years of our lives, weight being one example, our skin appearance being another, all our body is doing is reflecting information back to us. Usually, when we have gone through a lot of stress, illness, and built-up negative emotions, it shows a difference in our weight and skin appearance. Our bodies also change as a reflection of what we have experienced and our actions. It's all simply information, and that is it! When we put judgements and labels on the information, then it becomes an issue regarding our confidence, self-esteem, and self-love. Self-love is about feeling at home with ourselves no matter what judgements we have. The less judgement we can have of the information our body is giving to us, the better.

What judgements have you been making about the information your body is providing? When I talk about information, I'm not necessarily saying we can always make sense of what our body is telling us. Sometimes we just need to surrender to it. In time we can understand what it has all meant. It took me time to understand why I was experiencing the stomach pains for so long. Discovering it was my body holding on to the pain of abandonment and my worthiness beliefs.

We are not our bodies

You are not your body – let's repeat that – you are not your body! I believe our body is our vessel to express our spirit/soul through a unique self-expression vehicle that gets us from place to place. It's also the only place we have to move around and experience life with. My amazing friend, Sonya Furlong, has written and produced a song that beautifully expresses this message that we are not our bodies, our minds or whatever we may think we are. She sings, *you're a sweet spirit soul*. You can access this song at https://music.youtube.com/watch?v=_qwVmpKWKVY

We can see our core beliefs about life when we teach a child a concept, as we need to think carefully about what we want our children to know. With my darling three-year-old daughter, we lost a dear family member who was very close to her, her pops, and my dad-in-love (in-law). Explaining where he is now after he has passed had me sharing with her how we all have a soul and how this soul or spirit lives on and can watch over us forever. Now try explaining what a soul is to a three-year-old. I really had to think about what having a soul meant to me and what it means to be more than our bodies. I found myself saying, 'Your soul is your entire being.'

My three-year-old then thought about this and pointed to different body parts. She would point to her tummy and say, 'Is this my soul?' and I would reply, 'Well, not exactly, my darling!' We had a great big laugh when she proceeded to touch different parts of her body and asked again, 'Is this my soul?' I clarified, 'Your soul is who you really are.' She then pointed to her hand, and as she pointed to the palm of her hand, holding this perfect little hand up in my face, it came to me instantly how best to explain to her that she is not her body. While at the same time honouring how important her body is.

Thanks to my daughter, I can best explain how we can truly appreciate we are more than our bodies, while honouring and respecting our bodies for the magic vessels of our spirit they truly are.

Picture now yourself as a gorgeous three-year-old, pointing to the little palm of your hand and asking a loving guardian who knows all about divine wisdom and is here to share knowledge with you, about your spirit and body. You ask her, 'Is this my soul?' and she replies, 'This is your hand, for which you will care and give to others, whilst also nurturing yourself. You will use these hands to express yourself; through them, your warmth and ability to connect physically with others can occur. These capabilities, through your warm and loving hands, are your soul. Your soul can be expressed through your hands.'

Next, your three-year-old self points to her tummy, saying, 'Is this my soul?' Your wise guardian replies, 'Your tummy holds so much of your wisdom and power. It is the place of your body which is your centre, and you can come back to it at any point to realise your truth and what action to take next. If you truly listen to how it feels in your centre, you will be immediately connected to what is best for you. This is your soul guiding you.' You are in awe at just three years old, and it makes more and more sense, understanding how your body is the instrument you get to play with and how it expresses who you really are.

Another way to understand the above, our soul expressed in each different body part, is through our energy bodies. Known as our chakra system. I will outline the chakra system later in this chapter.

So, when did we stop being in awe of our bodies? When did we lose touch with simply using our bodies freely and expressively, just like we all did when we were young? We tend to forget our magic and stop using our bodies wisely when we take it for granted. We listen more to society about how our bodies should be instead of listening to our own bodies' magnificent magical wisdom. It is time to change this!

Accepting how we are now whilst being open to change and improvement

I can hear some readers thinking, 'Well, Lauren, how do I get past feeling so negative about how I look now and not feeling good about myself?' Remember, the outside world has created many messages that are sadly consistent with the idea beauty comes in only certain forms. And anything that does not fit with what we are shown is therefore not beautiful. We must see through these messages and realise they all lead back to selling products that wouldn't sell if the message was 'You are perfect, just as you are now.' They don't lead us to that truth because we would be less influenced to want to buy their products, such as diet regimes, supplements, skincare, makeup, and clothes, if we knew it.

Imagine if we loved and accepted ourselves first and foremost. Just as we are right now. Then from an overflow of that love, we felt drawn to certain things only because they felt best for us. Imagine if we weren't influenced by buying things not because we don't feel good about ourselves but because we already love and are grateful for our bodies. We would then buy with the intention of what will make us feel happy simply because we want to look after our health with diets, supplements, skincare, makeup, or clothes we are drawn to with our intuition. Not because we were influenced mindlessly on something that isn't the best for everybody only because we felt so insecure and disempowered.

Beauty is being you and being grateful for what your body does for you. It can also mean that it's a good thing to want to change, too. If you feel it will improve your health, because we should all value our health over what we look like; this is a lie we have been told through messaging that our bodies need to be slim to look good. But goodness, even being slim in certain ways can be unhealthy too. Therefore, we must make decisions from love and gratitude for our bodies and nothing else. When we come from love and appreciation, making the healthiest decisions which are right for us will be much easier. We feel energised and healthy when we can make the right choices.

Let's look at the diagrams below to see how acceptance whilst making changes is better than disliking and feeling disgusted towards our bodies:

The Disliking Self Cycle

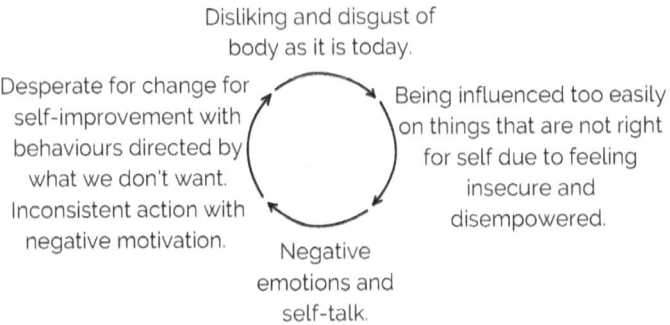

The Acceptance Self Cycle

Negative and positive motivation

You will notice in the diagrams above, the third stages are behaviours either directed by what we don't or do want. In the Disliking Self Cycle, it says, 'directed by what we don't want' and 'inconsistent action with negative motivation.' What does this mean? When we focus on what we don't want, which comes from negative emotions, negative self-talk and limiting beliefs about ourselves, this creates motivation that is driven by the negative. It's also called moving away from, as it is moving away from pain.

Examples are: I want to lose weight. I don't want my skin to have pimples and wrinkles. I don't want to look fat in my clothes. I don't want to be ugly. I don't want to be tired. These thoughts are focused on moving away from what we don't want. Knowing what we *don't want* is helpful to kickstart us into action. But when we continue to be driven by the negative, it creates inconsistent behaviours and results.

As an example, if we focus on losing weight, once some results have been achieved, and weight has been lost, it is easy to default back to old patterns of behaviour because there is now less motivation to keep doing the new behaviours. This becomes yo-yo dieting. We lose the weight, only to put it back on again and become motivated only when there is weight to lose. A similar example is with money - if we are motivated to make money to pay off debts, once any debt is paid off, motivation decreases. So, we overspend the money again just to find our motivation once we have more debt. We can only create consistent behaviours and results when we are driven by *how good it feels* to have more of what we want. Like being a healthier weight and to enjoy the food and exercise we choose. Or to earn more than we need and to keep focussing on how great it is to have an abundance of money.

In the Acceptance Self Cycle, it says, 'behaviours directed by what we want' and 'consistent action with positive motivation.' So, when we focus on all the great reasons why we want to have what we want, once we start showing results, we are continually driven to keep it up. To have even more of what we want. We don't stop the skincare regime once we have one good month of beautiful, glowing skin. Instead, we enjoy our skincare routine because we choose to look after our skin long-term. Or we continue to focus on all the great feelings and results we now have thanks to how we eat and move our bodies. Instead of being motivated by the things we don't want, like extra weight and tiredness, we focus on the positive of feeling slim, healthy, and energetic.

Give me more of that, please, thanks unconscious mind!

You will find my Acceptance Self Cycle at www.laurenjobson.com/bookfreecourse where you can print it out and remind yourself to focus on all the good things improving your behaviours can give you. Feeling good along the journey by accepting and loving how you are now creates more positivity today and in the future.

Our body wisdom and our sacred feminine - Storing memories and emotions in the body

In my own story, my body was screaming at me through the messenger of painful stomach aches. This was a powerful way of sending me a message. It let me eventually know how to listen to it and decode what it wanted me to know. With some guidance into my unconscious mind, the part of me that runs my body and the feminine side of receiving and listening to my body's wisdom. It was able to show me my 'not good enough and not lovable enough' beliefs that were being stored in my stomach, causing me pain.

It is in connecting with our feminine body wisdom where we can find all our answers and past emotions and beliefs. Let's explore this concept by understanding the chakra system and specifically bringing them back to how all of this relates to self-love.

We have seven main chakras that run up our spine. They are spirals of energy which receive, generate, and project energy. We have all had the experience of picking up the energy of someone, and it is the chakra energy we are referring to without us even knowing this. Chakras are unconscious to us and are described as holding on to images and memories we are storing in our bodies and projecting them out through our energy.

For example, in my story, I was storing my unresolved little girl who felt abandoned by her biological father in my energy field. Since my older self was not rescuing her from those emotions and beliefs, my energy was entwined with that powerlessness.

When we hold something in our energy for an extended time, it becomes such a strong pattern it is imprinted to be held firmly in our bodies. My body was restricted and holding on to the pain of not feeling good enough for who I am. Consequently, and relatively accurately, the chakra located in the stomach area is all about our power centre. My power centre of who I was and my relationship to my worthiness had imprinted firmly in my power chakra. My body played out this pattern with pain in my stomach. The more I had the pain, the more powerless I would feel, and it became a self-perpetuating cycle of a pattern playing out in my unconscious mind. The physical pain, to be clear, was very real. It was the cause of the pain that sat hidden in the unconscious mind, which is the part of us that runs our bodies.

As I mentioned before, our unconscious mind beats our heart, blinks our eyes, digests our food, regenerates every cell, and so on. It communicates to our Higher Self, which is connected to The Source to which we are all connected. It is from our Higher Self where we have a blueprint of our ideal health. The question is, if we don't have perfect health, why not? My answer to this is that we are humans living through imperfect experiences. Because of this, we all create blocks such as limiting beliefs about ourselves, having negative emotions and a multitude of influences and messages outside of us, confusing our connection to what is most ideal for our body and health. The more we can become aware of and clear these blockages of energy, the more we can tune in to our next level of health and self-love.

Let's break each chakra down now and see examples of how they receive, generate, and project energy according to their location in our body.

Our energy bodies – The Chakra System

You may have been introduced to the chakra system before,

or this may be new to you. If it is new, I encourage you to read up on them if you find this interesting or would like to understand this more deeply. The more I learn about them, I discover how much they make sense. I love how different people and ways of thinking explain them.

One of my favourite explanations of them is in the book *Spirit Babies, How to Communicate with the Child You're Meant to Have* by Walter Makichen. He was a clairvoyant and could pick up a lot of information about a person from what he saw in people's energy fields. I love how he describes chakras, "Chakras give us a way to reach from the physical world into the soul's realm." He describes them as a system that links body, mind, and spirit by connecting us to our energy of potential, more commonly called our soul.

A profound read and detailed resource is the book, *Anatomy of The Spirit* written by Caroline Myss. In fact, it was a Caroline Myss book I was reading on the train that day which I shared in my introduction. She was one of the first authors and leaders in the field of Personal Development, to influence my love for this industry.

One more fantastic recommendation for information on the chakras, is from an incredible woman, Antoniette Gomez, by who I was certified as a Chakra Mindset Trainer. She is a dear friend too, and her work is called *Chakra Mindset*. She has a book and a journal you can learn through. You can order these by doing a Google search of her name and *Chakra Mindset* (*link to purchase also in References at back of this book*).

Instead of me asking you to look at your physical body for any ailments and go into the physical realm, we will look at the emotions and beliefs in each area. Books like Carolyn Myss's mentioned above, Louise L. Hay's book *You Can Change Your Life* and Annette Noontil's book The *Body is the Barometer of the Soul* are great for exploring the link between emotions and beliefs and how they can show up in the body. Once you become aware of any limiting beliefs in any chakra, you can explore how your body could be holding onto and reflecting information.

For each of the chakras, I have created a Self-Love Principle, and from them, I will have us do a 'body gratitude check' to see if we can become conscious of any blockages of energy, limitations or things holding us back in this area of our life. The more we can be grateful for what our body does for us, the more we will deepen our self-love, taking us beyond anything like our appearance.

The 7 Different Levels to Deepen Our Self-Love: Our Chakra System

Chakra One – The Base Chakra

It is located around the area of our sexual organs and includes our legs, the base of the spine, feet, and the immune system.

Lauren's Self-Love Principle for this Chakra:
Do I love myself enough to be grounded in my body and to respect my relationship with the physical realm eg. my health, finances and environments like home and office? Have I created a space in my life where I feel like I belong?

The main theme is: Looking after our physical health, our financial health and our relationship to our external environment. Feeling safe, supported, trusting, and like we belong. It is also about our ability to provide for life's necessities.

This chakra is about the foundation of life and how we are grounded in our bodies and relationship to this earth.

Note: Although I explain the seven chakras in order here first, they are explored in greater detail in the chapters which follow in a different order. This is because I needed to share how to understand and implement other essential concepts first.

Body gratitude check. Here are some questions to reflect on for this chakra:

What do I believe about my ability to look after all my basic needs, such as financial security, health, and creating an environment to feel safe in and where I belong?

_____

_____

_____

_____

When I think of the Self-Love Principle for this chakra and my beliefs above, what emotions do I have?

_____

_____

_____

_____

Can I notice and be grateful for my body, which allows me to create money and a place where I belong? Can I be grateful for experiencing health in my body? Why or why not?

_____

_____

_____

_____

Chakra Two – The Sacral Chakra

It is located around the stomach area between our belly button and sexual organs.

Lauren's Self-Love Principle for this Chakra:
Do I love myself enough to master my emotions and enjoy pleasure?

The main theme is: Learning to master our emotions and respect receptivity. This is our relationship to our emotions and self-worth.

This chakra is all about our wants and desires, shown through our emotions. Chakra one is all about our needs, and this one is all about our wants. We need to learn how to receive in our lives as it is a loving thing to do for ourselves and others. Nothing is loving about pushing away someone's compliments or gifts because it takes away the feeling for them of the gift of giving.

In Chapter Eight, I talk in more depth about the power and importance of receptivity as a self-loving principle.

Body gratitude check. Here are some questions to reflect on for this chakra:

What do I believe about my ability to receive pleasure and what I desire in life? Am I willing to sit with my emotions, express them positively and learn from them?

_____
_____
_____
_____

When I think of the Self-Love Principle for this chakra and my beliefs above, what emotions do I have?

_____
_____
_____
_____

Can I notice and be grateful for my body, which allows me to feel deeply and completely? And to enjoy receiving desires and pleasure? Why or why not?

_____
_____
_____
_____

Chakra Three – The Solar Plexus Chakra

It is located around our centre, from our belly button to the breastbone.

Lauren's Self-Love Principle for this Chakra:
Do I love myself enough to look after my boundaries and stand up for what is important to me?

The main theme is: Knowing and honouring our boundaries with effective communication. This is our relationship to our personal power and confidence.

This chakra is about communicating with ourselves and others about what is best for us. Discerning what is good for us and what to let go of. This is about honouring our boundaries by knowing them for ourselves, sticking to them and effectively communicating our needs to others. It's our place of personal power and confidence.

Chapter Four in this book is all about this chakra.

Body gratitude check. Here are some questions to reflect on for this chakra:

What do I believe about my ability to set boundaries with others, such as being able to say no to things I don't want to do?

_____
_____
_____
_____

When I think of the Self-Love Principle for this chakra and my beliefs above, what emotions do I have?

_____
_____
_____
_____

Can I notice and be grateful for my body, which allows me to connect to my power through messages from my gut and body wisdom? Why or why not?

_____
_____
_____
_____

Chakra Four – The Heart Chakra.

It is located around our heart.

Lauren's Self-Love Principle for this Chakra:
Do I love myself enough to have relationships with a loving connection to myself and others?

The main theme is: Our relationship with love and the people in our life. It is how we share unconditional love, empathy, and compassion. Do we invite loving and supportive people into our lives?

This chakra is about how we live from our heart by listening to it, following it and sharing it with others. The next chapter, Chapter Three, is about living aligned with our highest values, by the guiding light of our heart. What are our heart's highest priorities?

I go into depth with this chakra in Chapter Three.

Body gratitude check. Here are some questions to reflect on for this chakra:

What do I believe about my ability to be in and sustain supportive and loving relationships?

_____

_____

_____

_____

When I think of the Self-Love Principle for this chakra and my beliefs above, what emotions do I have?

_____

_____

_____

_____

Can I notice and be grateful for my body, which allows me to give and receive love to others? Why or why not?

_____

_____

_____

_____

Chakra Five – The Throat Chakra

It is located around our throat.

Lauren's Self-Love Principle for this Chakra:
Do I love myself enough to communicate my needs, wants and speak up for what is important to me?

The main theme is: Our relationship to using our voice by knowing what we stand for as a person and the ability we have to express ourselves. It is the creative and spiritual expression of our voices with the continual question we can ask ourselves; are we using our words to ourselves and others wisely?

This chakra is about self-expression on all the levels we can have; physically, mentally, emotionally, and spiritually. Do we express our needs effectively?

Do we have intellectual, respectful, and mature conversations with others? Can we express our emotions effectively when we need to? Do we connect with a message with what we believe in and feel confident to share it as our contribution?

Chapter Six is all about this chakra.

Body gratitude check. Here are some questions to reflect on for this chakra:

What do I believe about my ability to communicate my needs to others and to speak up, even if my point of view is different to others?

_____
_____
_____
_____

When I think of the Self-Love Principle for this chakra and my beliefs above, what emotions do I have?

_____
_____
_____
_____

Can I notice and be grateful for my body, which allows me to have a voice and express myself through my body? Why or why not?

_____
_____
_____
_____

Chakra Six – The Third Eye Chakra

It is located around our third eye, which is in between and just above our eyebrows.

Lauren's Self-Love Principle for this Chakra:
Do I love myself enough to listen to and follow my intuition?

The main theme is: Our relationship and connection to our intuition.

This chakra is all about our inner wise one, our intuition. It is about learning to listen more effectively and deeply to this part of us. Do we trust our intuition and hear it in the first place when it speaks? It is about seeing things from a higher perspective. It is also our relationship to follow our gut instinct in our power centre near our stomach and in our third eye, which connects to our all-knowing.

I have some tips on connecting better, listening, and following our intuition in Chapter Seven.

Body gratitude check. Here are some questions to reflect on for this chakra:

What do I believe about my ability to listen to and follow my intuition?

_____
_____
_____
_____

When I think of the Self-Love Principle for this chakra and my beliefs above, what emotions do I have?

_____
_____
_____
_____

Can I notice and be grateful for my body, which allows me to connect to my intuition? Why or why not?

_____
_____
_____
_____

Chakra Seven – The Crown Chakra

It is located at the top and centre of our head.

Lauren's Self-Love Principle for this Chakra:
Do I love myself enough to feel at one with all, and have a deep connection to something bigger than myself?

The main theme is: Our relationship with a deeper meaning to life where we know how we fit in and belong in this world.

This chakra is about our soul's purpose, connection to universal consciousness and spirituality. Spirituality can mean any beliefs you may have that take you beyond this physical realm of our five senses. For some, it could be a religion. For others, it could be one belief that has them feel there is a bigger purpose and meaning to our physical existence. It is entirely personal and is all about having inner authority – meaning you can respect a higher being yet still feel you are the one responsible for and in control of your life.

I focus on this chakra in Chapter Seven with this ambiguous and profound concept.

Body gratitude check. Here are some questions to reflect on for this chakra:

What do I believe about my ability to have a purpose bigger than my own personal needs and making a contribution to others?

_____
_____
_____
_____

When I think of the Self-Love Principle for this chakra and my beliefs above, what emotions do I have?

_____
_____
_____
_____

Can I notice and be grateful for my body, which allows me to have a connection to something bigger than me? Why or why not?

_____
_____
_____
_____

Another fabulous read on chakras with a creative spin is a book called *The Seven Chakra Sisters, Make Friends with the Inner Allies Who Keep You Healthy, Laughing, Loving and Wise*, by Linda Linker Rosenthal. I love how she names the Chakra Sisters with their key natures. For example, the First Sister for the First Chakra is called 'Aneeda' as this Root Chakra is all about our basic needs being met, and it's a play on 'I need a.' The Seventh Chakra, the Crown Chakra, is named 'Iamone' as this is all about the collective consciousness, 'I am one.' It's a fun and insightful read.

Conclusion of this vow

I vow to love my body.
I honour the relationship I have with the home I get to live and experience life through.

With all of the chakras in mind now, I will cover each of them in depth through the chapters. They inform a holistic approach to our relationship with ourselves. We need to understand how we are not just our physical bodies. If we can live with this belief that we are so much more than what we see and perceive of our physical self, we can deepen our self-love by appreciating all the layers that make up who we are.

Let's work through each layer by going through this book and making a self-loving commitment that you will forevermore work on this most precious and enduring relationship; the one you have with yourself.

A summary of what you learned in Chapter Two

I Vow to Love My Body.

I honour the relationship I have with the home
I get to live and experience life through.

- Lauren's story on having seven half-siblings
- Our relationship to our body - Body image is ours for the making
- We are not our bodies
- Accepting how we are now whilst being open to change and improvement
- Our body wisdom and our sacred feminine - Storing memories and emotions in the body
- Our energy bodies – The Chakra System

Devoting yourself to applying the learnings in this chapter:

1. Using the Self-Loving Resources of Tools and Mindset: Grab your journal or the workbook I created for you at www.laurenjobson.com/bookfreecourse. Ask yourself these powerful questions that were asked throughout this chapter and any others you want to add. Go within to listen to what answers come to you and write them down without judgement or questioning. No one else needs to see your answers so go ahead and deepen your connection to the relationship you have with your body.

2. Using the Self-Loving Resource of Support: A Matrix Therapies® and NLP Master Practitioner can help you remove any blocks such as limiting beliefs and emotions you might have become aware of from this chapter and the questions above.

3. Using the Self-Loving Resource of Creativity: Create future focussed, empowering and exciting affirmations for self in each chakra. This is similar to a goal setting exercise, and I have examples at www.laurenjobson.com/bookfreecourse

4. Using the Self-Loving Resource of Health: What do we have if we do not have our physical health? While we are focussing on loving our bodies, it is time to align our actions with creating and maintaining health. In the next chapter we learn how to elicit our values in an area of life. I highly recommend discovering your health values and work on creating behaviours (Chapter Nine) which improve health.

5. Using the Self-Loving Resource of Action: All of the information in this chapter could just be interesting theory until we devote ourselves to taking applied action. Answer the questions from this chapter and be sure to grab your journal and use the tool of my online course.

Chapter Three

I Vow to Live in Alignment with My Highest Values.

I honour the relationship I have with my heart's priorities.

Vow Three

"This above all: to thine own self be true."

WILLIAM SHAKESPEARE.

When I was 12 years old, I adamantly decided I would become a drummer when I went to high school the following year. Not just to learn to play the drums but to *become* a drummer. Becoming a drummer felt so inspiring, and there was a deep sense that learning to master this instrument would somehow bring me closer to myself.

I would get to school earlier than the usual starting time to be at band practice. I had my beloved drumsticks in hand and dedicated myself to becoming so good that I could have my own drum kit one day and totally rock out with amazing drum solos.

I did become that drummer I envisioned. It opened many amazing opportunities to express myself. Becoming a skilled drummer meant I ended up being the only one who could read drum notation in the school. Consequently, I played for the senior students' final music exams. One day, my lovely and proud music teacher handed me the school's credit card, telling me I could go and purchase anything I wanted for my own drum set to use for my exams. I loved this reward and received a high mark in music for the final exams because I was wholeheartedly dedicated, committed and devoted to becoming who I wanted to be.

When we were encouraged to start thinking about jobs or careers after graduating high school, I had absolutely no idea what I wanted to do. All I knew was that I would quickly put my hand up for leadership positions in the school. As well as my love for playing and listening to music. I was elected President of the Student Representative Council in Year Ten and then elected as School Captain for my final year. I found I loved doing speeches with inspiring quotes and sharing what I felt we were all going through as young girls and where we might like to see ourselves in the future. (Yes, I went to an all-girls school. I enjoyed it and think I would have been distracted by having boys around.)

With synchronicity, a family member had a connection to a CEO of a music record company. Since I needed to choose a place to do one week's work experience, I was invited to go and do it there. This week of work experience was one of the best weeks of my teenage years, if not *the best*. I loved it! I saw a band record a song in the studio. I went to a radio station with an artist, Pete Murray, to be with him for his interview on Triple J. I saw how recording artists had the production of their albums made from the cover's design, to the creation of their brand persona, and so much more. I still remember today feeling so happy and in awe of the 'real world' outside of high school.

This experience lit up my heart. I knew what I wanted to do when I grew up. I wanted to be in the music industry and work for a record label. I loved playing music as a drummer, but funnily enough, even though I became really good at the drums, I felt called to support other musicians on their journey. I continued to play to have fun and to help others through my drum tutoring.

I chose to go to a college where I could get an Advanced Diploma in Marketing, specialising in the Entertainment Industry. I did this because of the six months internship, which meant for two days a week, I would work with a company in the industry for the experience instead of money. It sure was an experience! Not always rainbows and happiness like I had dreamt it would be. Rather it felt like a test of my willingness to pursue what I thought I wanted. Sometimes I found it soul-crushing because I saw things misaligned with my values. I didn't fully grasp this discomfort at the time as not being aligned with my values. I would secretly cry at some things I saw. In my young life, seeing the world outside of school, I didn't yet realise why I felt so confused sometimes. When I looked back, I could see how my values directly conflicted with the external world I was experiencing.

There was still this part of me who really wanted to pursue this 'dream job'. With a lot of belief in myself and taking action to apply myself where necessary, I did land it. I was so excited! I started working for a record label.

I soon fitted in and loved the people I was working with. Part of my role was selling the CDs (remember those?) to music retailers across Australia, with artists from Red Hot Chili Peppers, Muse, Madonna and that year, even Paris Hilton's single. We were highly encouraged to go to the gigs to support our musicians. This meant about two to three times a week, some weeks even more often, going to the city to hear our bands play and welcome them to the label. Part of me absolutely loved the fun and excitement of this since I loved the music and felt so special connecting with the artists. I remember being at one of The Temper Trap's first small gigs before they became well-known. *Sweet Disposition* is one of my favourite songs of all time. Evermore was also a band close to us, and we saw the boys (an endearing label) perform and spoke to them often.

Another part of me felt so torn from what my body and heart wanted because attending each gig, after work and well into the night on our own time, meant that I didn't get to see much of my partner. It was utterly exhausting. Eventually, constantly going out most nights took a toll on my physical and mental health. As I look back, I probably had more choice than I felt. At the time, all I knew for sure was I could not deny my feelings that something was just *off* for me, and it wasn't going to light up my heart like I first thought it would.

I felt the true me was being crushed inside. This was no longer my dream. I no longer had a plan my heart called to. A deep part of me knew I had to create space for a new dream to be called in. I felt I had to get clear on why I was feeling this way to become confident with the decision I was about to make.

I sat down after work one day, asking myself what I really wanted in life. I wanted to have more time in the evenings to be with my partner (now my husband and father to my children). I also wanted to look after my health, get enough rest and have more time to work on myself and learn about human potential. I had no idea what to do next except tell my boss that I could no longer work there. So, I did. On my last day, I finally felt I was free and unencumbered. I trusted that whatever was next for me would happen. Even when I didn't have a clue what my future looked like.

This leads us to our next relationship to explore: the one we have to our heart's priorities.

Our relationship with our heart's priorities – our values

Values the world over are described as the things in life most important to us. The Oxford Languages dictionary will even tell us that values are principles or standards of behaviour, one's judgment of what is important in life.

Values are one of my favourite topics to teach in my NLP certification programs because I have seen time and time again how profound the insight gained, once becoming conscious of our heart's priorities. When my students and clients become aware of what drives them to achieve certain things, I see massive transformations when change occurs within their values.

We all have values, and we have them in priority lists of most important to least important for each area of our life. We also have a priority list for our core life values which are our deepest heart's desires, for our life in general. Values are usually unconscious until we truly think about them and bring them to our conscious awareness. We use our masculine energy to shine the light into our unconscious minds as we ask, 'What is most important to me in this area of my life or in my life?' By receiving the question to uncover our values, we use our feminine energy to reveal this previously unconscious part of us. This process, again, is our sacred marriage within.

Our values are what we hold most important to us as our highest priorities, our wishes, and the qualities we most expect from life. They shape how we live and feel about ourselves. They determine how we judge our actions and the actions of others. Values create our motivation. They make up a big part of who we are, as they underpin the ethics we live by and our morals. I call them our heart's priorities and our guiding lights for what we are motivated to fulfil.

Values are not the actions we take, such as going to the gym or the clothes we choose to wear. They are the needs and the meanings we put unconsciously to these actions. Such as, health could be the value behind the motivation to go to the gym. Or it could be the value of looking good to gain more confidence for someone else. The desire to buy and appreciate designer clothes could be driven by the value of luxury and having the best quality of things. For someone else, it could be their value of following trends to look good or to belong. You can see they are entirely personal and unique to each individual and cannot be recognised at face value for what we see on the surface of people's behaviour.

We value what we do primarily because of what we have experienced up until today. Values are formed by external influences such as key people in our lives, the environment we grew up in, both in a geographical sense and the family structure around us, the religion (if any) we were raised in, the schools we went to and now, more so than ever before, the information and media we consume. These all create what we make important today, until we choose to change them.

Below is an example of someone's core life values in order

of importance. This person was asked, 'What is important to you in your life?'

Example of Core Life Values:

1. Family - Whomever this person considers to be 'family.' This value will encompass all the important reasons why family is important to them. Such as love, connection, quality time, security, etc.
2. Community and Friends – This value could comprise of connection with others outside the family, companionship, sharing of love and resources, helping each other, and support.
3. Health – Feeling connected to the physical self, strong mind and body connection, energy, eating well, body movement, etc.
4. Making A Difference – Contributing something to the world to help others.
5. Passion and Purpose – Loving what they do as their contribution and feeling on path to sharing their unique gifts with others.
6. Fun – Enjoying life and receiving its pleasures.
7. Growth and Achievement – Feeling like a success and making progress towards personal and professional goals.
8. Creativity - Expressing ideas using their imagination.
9. Connection to Nature – Appreciating Mother Earth and respecting the land we live on.

You might look at the values above and notice you could relate to some of these and resonate with the explanations, too.

Or you could have similar values yet interpret them differently with your reasons as to why they are important to you. You may have completely different values to these and can have them in a different order of importance to the example above.

The order of importance that we rank our values, dramatically affects the results we attain in life too. If we want more of something in our lives because we feel we don't have enough of it – say, the value of fun, for example, it means it is not prioritised highly enough. Making change in the order of our values, changes our priorities and consequently our daily behaviours change too. I'll go over this later on in the chapter.

How do you find out your values?

A great way to become conscious of your values, for your core life values or if you want to get clear on a specific area of your life, is to think about your life in general, or this area of life you want to explore, and ask yourself:

'In the last three months, what have I spent most of my time doing? And what have I spent my money on?' The answers to these questions will give you a lot of insight.

If you focus on life in general, you would be considering what you have spent time and money on, and notice how you will have about two or three areas of life that have a lot more priority over others. Over our lives, our values change according to what the environment asks of us. It might be things like the area of health or your contribution through work have been your priorities. Then, when a significant change happens, like wanting a life partner and children or wanting to travel the world, your environment changes and thus our priorities will also change or adjust accordingly. For some, it could be they now need to look after an elderly parent, or they become a parent themselves. At times like these, values would need to adjust to the new environment of their life.

If you focus on just one area of life, like health, you see what you have prioritised in your health. You may notice you have spent so much money wanting to do more exercise and on organic, healthy food. Yet, your time might show how you have prioritised other things, like spending more time with friends and family over going to the gym and cooking food at home. We can quickly see if we have a conflict in values as we honour one value but disregard another. This can be common. I will explain further below.

Have you been spending time and money aligned with what you say and think is most important to you, or can you see you have valued other things instead?

If we reflect on a recent time of our lives, whether it is the last three months, six months, or twelve months, and we realise we are not happy with where we have been spending our time and money, we need to look at how our six core human needs have been motivating us.

Fulfilling core human needs with unresourceful behaviours

Why is it that we engage in self-destructive behaviour and

can spend so much time and money doing so? How could this show us our values?

Since we only ever spend time and money on what is important to us, we might need to look deeper for the purpose we are endeavouring to fulfil. When the surface level of behaviour is not self-loving, there is generally an underlying, unconscious purpose: our value, that is wanting to be fulfilled. If we can become aware of what we are striving to make important, we can then re-evaluate our behaviours to become aligned with what we deeply want.

For instance, watching a lot of TV or scrolling our phones for too long, we might notice how unresourceful this behaviour is becoming. As it becomes an unhealthy habit and starts to no longer feel enjoyable, we could ask; what am I striving to fulfill? What is important to me about watching TV or scrolling my phone?

The value could be enjoying life, resting, having fun, escaping to rest my thoughts etc. It could be the deeper value of safety and security since at least we feel safe in our habits because they are familiar.

Engaging in behaviours that feel good to us in the moment but are not good for us, means we might start to sacrifice other, more important values. When we do this, we are prioritising feeling good in the short term to the detriment of such things as health and connection with family, for example. It is likely we are fulfilling a core human need but in a way which has us prioritise a habit over finding a more resourceful way to fulfill the same need.

There are six core human needs:

1. Safety and Security
2. Love and Connection
3. Certainty
4. Variety

Once these four physical needs are met, people can strive to fulfil their need for

5. Growth
6. Contribution

Suppose the value underneath the behaviour of watching TV is to enjoy life, or safety and certainty, yet it is not good for our health, we can ask, 'What else could I do that is healthier for me, which will make me feel I am enjoying life, while feeling safe and certain?' The answers to this could be reading a book, meditating, listening to soft music, cuddling with my partner or pet, and so on.

Another example is, for many, being on social media is a way for people to fulfil love and connection to others. I think it can start out as this value, most of the time, but it can easily become a mind-numbing habit of scrolling for fear of missing out on someone else's news – even if that someone is a complete stranger in 'real life.' The irony is in having the habit of being attached to our phones for the unconscious fulfilment of love and connection, we can become disconnected from those most important to us, such as our children, partner or even our closest friends. It is time to become more conscious of what first inspired our behaviours but has become completely misaligned with the higher intent we want to be fulfilled.

This is like sacrificing long-term, higher priorities for short-term satisfaction. Sometimes, our heart wants us to value a particular thing, like health, yet our unconscious programming and unresolved pains from the past have us carrying out behaviours entirely misaligned with what we really want. We can get stuck in habits which become unhealthy for us.

I knew a lovely Italian man who learnt NLP and went to coaching because he was obese for most of his life, and he really wanted to be healthy and slimmer. Being Italian, in his family values, were to get together, and his mum would cook up big carbohydrate-heavy meals of pasta and pizza with big servings, too. When he discovered this concept of values, he uncovered his deep unconscious value of belonging and connection to his family. A core human need of love and connection.

Once we uncover our values, we also notice how we have certain beliefs attached to a value. He became aware of his unconscious belief about how he felt eating his mother's food, even if he didn't want to eat the big portions, equalled love for his mother. That somehow, if he didn't eat all of what she made him, it wouldn't show her his love in the same way. In this example, the deeper and more important value of love, belonging and connection to his family and mother, overruled his value of being healthy. He was prioritising a perceived need of someone else over his health. We could then guide him to understand how he could continue to belong, love and be connected to his family whilst still eating what he really wanted and doing what was best for his health. He realised he could show his mother love while not eating the same food or at least, not eating all of it. He did become healthy and slim and has maintained great health ever since.

To understand this possibility of how we could be doing this in our own lives, let's look into what I mean by being in alignment with our heart's priorities.

What is alignment?

Alignment means to be in the 'proper positioning' in relation to each other. If someone values health yet behaves in ways that are not healthy, this is not alignment.

If something in your life does not feel right to you and is creating negative emotions such as sadness, anger, shame, guilt, dislike, regret or such, then if you ask, 'What is important to me about this that is causing me to feel this way?' The answer can show you how your values are most likely misaligned. It is the essence of what is happening, the meaning you are putting to such an event that is causing you to feel positive or negative about it - and your values determine your experience of it and the meaning you are creating.

For example, someone might value connection with friends and family, and there might be times when they get so busy, they don't see or talk to them very often. This person may feel guilty and unfulfilled like something is missing. If we are misaligned with our values, we feel depressed, unmotivated, lost, overwhelmed and unfulfilled, like something is missing. Chances are, the things we feel are missing are most likely the fulfilment of our values. It becomes worthwhile to discover what is important to us, to align our behaviours accordingly.

Our values are our guiding lights. The closer we are to fulfilling our values through our behaviours, the more in alignment to them we become. We feel happy, passionate, proud, and most authentically ourselves. We can feel purposeful and satisfied with the results we are getting in our life.

Therefore, our true values are essential to know. When we are conscious of our values for each area of our lives, we can intentionally create more and more ways in our daily lives to be driven by them, act in accordance with them, live aligned with our heart's desires and feel truly fulfilled.

How our values and beliefs are interconnected

At the most unconscious level, our heart values what it does because of our beliefs about why these things are important to us. Growing up, we pick up all sorts of beliefs about everything. In our beliefs, we create values. As we move into adulthood, we can rebel against formed values and adopt new values simply because we have choices, new beliefs, and independence.

As I've mentioned, values sit behind the actions, so for example, with going to the gym, the value could be anything from looking good, protecting our health, having energy, competition, winning, or fitting in with others. With all these different reasons why someone values going to the gym, there is a belief or a set of beliefs determining why this is important to them.

Let's say a person experiences a lot of pain and struggle in the area of intimate relationships. They might then believe intimate relationships are not worth getting into and are too much work. Because of this belief, they then stop valuing an intimate relationship as much as they do other areas of their lives. So suddenly, they start to value and prioritise working on their career as more important than dating. They could also focus on their health, home and social life, finances, and spirituality. Before they know it, they are keeping themselves so busy they no longer prioritise dating or intimate relationships at all.

That is, until they realise they now want to have an intimate partner. Focussing on intimate relationships, they may continue to feel negative about themselves from past experiences. Here is a place of growth, a place where they can learn so much about themselves because by placing a priority on this area again, it will mean they need to confront their feelings, attitudes, and beliefs to work on manifesting what they want.

When I looked at how I wanted to make more money in my business, I elicited my business values. I discovered, as we would have guessed, I wasn't prioritising making money over other things such as helping people, doing a good job, and loving what I do. I needed to explore my beliefs about money. Any limiting beliefs about making money, I resolved with my coach. As a result, my unconscious mind could give making money a higher importance inside of my business values. As I asked my unconscious mind what it is I then value in my business going forward, I had created a new value of marketing myself. My inner wisdom, after resolving the money beliefs that weren't serving me, created this value of showing up and marketing myself because this was an important way to make more money. This is the power of exploring our values and interconnected beliefs. We do this at the NLP Master

Practitioner Training, and I help my clients do this too.

Self-love is living in alignment with what we hold as most important in our hearts and having supportive beliefs about ourselves with each value. It is eye opening to uncover our beliefs which are driving our behaviours at an unconscious level. We can then consciously choose more empowering beliefs and find that our behaviours change accordingly.

Conclusion of this vow

I vow to live in alignment with my highest values.
I honour the relationship I have with my heart's priorities.

It is also worthwhile to notice when there is an imbalance of time and energy spent in just one area of life. I see a lot of escapism happening when there is such an imbalance it has become an addiction. I see a lot of people who come to me for coaching because they can't find or maintain intimate relationships or reach their career goals. A pattern I have seen is they have become addicted to going to the gym. The area of health for them is so much of their focus, if they feel a partner will be in the way of their meal planning, they won't stay with the person anymore. An addiction to going to the gym has been a detriment to other areas of their life. I believe it is because there is a sense of certainty and safety (at the deepest level of motivation) since they can control what they do and the results they can get. It is a promised outcome. If they do the work, they will get the results. Compared to in relationships, there is uncertainty and less control of the outcome. When we see this, it is time to explore the beliefs inside of the person's values.

Follow your heart. When we are out of alignment with our values, we can create a lot of drama and stories we tell ourselves about how it isn't easy to get what we want. We only have a certain amount of time each day. If we are spending our time and money on lower priorities, the things we want to make important in our lives, stay elusive to us.

Knowing what is most important in our lives and taking the right actions to fulfil our values requires us to have healthy beliefs about ourselves and the areas we want to improve. It may take vulnerability and conscious intention at first, but it is oh-so worth it! This is another aspect of self-love.

Let your values be a guide and act in a way that will help you align with them. For anything you find yourself doing, particularly any habits, continue to ask yourself; 'What am I making important right here in this precious moment? Is it of value to me and if not, how can I change this to fulfil my heart's true priorities?'

A summary of what you learned in
Chapter Three

I Vow to Live in Alignment with My Highest Values.

**I honour the relationship I have
with my heart's priorities.**

- Lauren's story on the music industry and her dream job
- Our relationship with our heart's priorities – our values
- How do you find out your values?
- Fulfilling core human needs with unresourceful behaviours
- The six core human needs
- What is alignment?
- How our values and beliefs are interconnected

Devoting yourself to applying the learnings in this chapter:

1. Using the Self-Loving Resources of Tools and Mindset: Grab your journal or my workbook I created for you at www.laurenjobson.com/bookfreecourse

Ask yourself these powerful questions and any others you want to add. Go within to listen to what answers come to you and write them down without judgement or questioning. No one else needs to see your answers so go ahead and deepen your connection to your heart and unconscious mind by practising the act of simply listening and acknowledging your wisdom within.

Q1. 'In the last three months, what have I spent most of my time doing, and what have I spent my money on?' The answers to these questions will give you a lot of insight into what your core life values are.

Q2. Pick an area of life or think about life in general and ask yourself: 'What is important to me in this area of my life?' or 'What is important to me in life?'

Q3. Have you been spending time and money aligned with what you say, and think is most important to you? Or can you see if you have valued other things instead?

Q4. For anything you find yourself doing, particularly any habits, continue to ask yourself; 'What am I making important right here in this precious moment? Is it of value to me? If not, how can I change this to fulfil my heart's true priorities?'

2. Using the Self-Loving Resources of Support and Environment: A Matrix Therapies® and NLP Master Practitioner can help you remove any blocks such as limiting beliefs and emotions you might have become aware of from this chapter and the questions above.

Also, the support from your external environment is important here. Look around what you have in your environments which include your home, office, car and anything you carry around with you on a daily basis. Your environment is showing you what you have been valuing. Declutter anything in your environments which no longer serves you. Think about what you want to make less important, such as keeping your phone out of your bedroom, and invite more of what you want to prioritise into your everyday life. If you want to read more, have your books handy. Allow your environment to work for you and support you.

3. Using the Self-Loving Resource of Action: All of this information in this chapter could just be interesting theory until we devote ourselves to taking applied action. Answer the questions from this chapter and be sure to grab your journal and use the tool of my online course.

4. Using the Self-Loving Resource of Forgiveness: This is a reminder that life and self-love is a process. Do what you feel drawn to and practise forgiveness. Particularly self-forgiveness. I also like EFT (emotional freedom technique) for forgiveness as the script is beautiful: "Even though I (state problem), I deeply and completely, love and accept myself". I will share resources on how to do this in my online course at www.laurenjobson.com/bookfreecourse. Again, doing Matrix Therapies® is also wonderful for the practise of forgiveness.

Chapter Four

I Vow to Make Self-Loving Decisions.

I honour the relationship I have with my power.

"Happiness lies in the cultivation of the garden."

VOLTAIRE

The phone-throwing incident with my father was the end of him being my father at all. After saying goodbye to my sisters and travelling to make a home in Australia; we had to say one more difficult goodbye. It was to some special neighbours. Across the road from where we lived was a lovely elderly couple. It was this family who my mum reached out to and was trying to call the day my father came back home from being with another woman. They were a tremendous source of support for my mum when she had me.

My mum told me about the time I wouldn't stop crying and she didn't know what to do. She went across the road and Morfydd, the daughter of this couple was there. This gentle and straight talking woman, (in her English accent) asked my mum, "Are you trying to cook your child?" I had many layers on, due to mum being worried I would be cold from the snow outside. Morfydd gently took off the layers to Mum's relief that was all it was. She had a son, who worked in the Royal Airforce (RAF) and was away for long periods. When he could come home from his duty at the RAF, he would visit his grandparents.

Over the years, Mum became acquainted with him due to his regular visits to see them.

His name was John and he fancied Mum. He asked her on a few dates before we left the country. Mum gave him our new address where we would be living in Australia as we were moving in with her parents, (my beloved Nan and Grandad) and her little brother (my uncle Simon) in a leafy suburb called Turramurra in Sydney. Her sister, my Aunty Annie, had moved out of home by then.

John wrote Mum letters for months and she wrote back. I would call them love letters. One day, John surprised us by appearing in Australia, with the hope of asking Mum out on more dates. He hadn't come to Australia for any other reason. A few dates later they went on an evening cruise on Sydney's Darling Harbour.

As the sun was setting, just as the boat was sailing underneath the Sydney Harbour Bridge, John got down on one knee and asked Mum, 'Nik, will you do me the honour of becoming my wife and allowing me to become Lauren's Father?'

She said "Yes!" John has been my true dad ever since. Also, the lovely neighbours across the road from my first home, the daughter of the elderly couple, Morfydd and her husband, became my beloved and treasured Grandparents, Abuela and Grandad. That straight talking woman who saved me from being 'cooked' (through no true fault of my mum, thank you Mum for making sure I was warm!) has been my Abuela ever since. (Abuela is Spanish for Grandma since she didn't want to be called Grandma for her fear of sounding old. My Grandad was of Spanish heritage.)

I loved hearing how Dad bought not only a return ticket

back to England for himself but for Mum and I too. He was that hopeful. I love his dedication to following his heart. I'd say I gained that from him.

I was the flower girl at my parents wedding when I was two. We travelled around with my dad wherever he was stationed, which included Germany and Wales. I have fond memories of them taking me to see castles, including the one made famous by the movie *Chitty Chitty Bang Bang*. My relationship with my Grandparents grew as they loved me just as much as if I was their biological granddaughter. They always have.

Just after my fourth birthday, my little sister was born in Wales. We moved back to Australia when I was five. My little brother was born when I was seven years old. I grew up in Australia, with my parents in love and being the eldest of three. I had my happy family, after all.

My mum would sometimes show me old photos of a man who she told me was my biological father. I kind of knew what she meant, as there were photos of him cuddling me as a baby. It didn't really mean much to me, whilst I was young, because I already had a dad. These photo albums I liked to look through also showed my older sisters, the dogs we had in the backyard where we lived together, and the holiday we took together in Australia. My mum would tell me all about them and always said I could ask her any questions. I found it really interesting, yet I didn't quite know what it meant to me. I felt secure in my family, being the oldest of three. It felt like, if I thought deeply about this prospect of having other siblings, well then I wouldn't quite know how I fitted into a different family arrangement.

With hindsight, I believe it was when I was a young teenager that I started to accept I had other siblings. It was the beginning of me questioning how I fitted into this new family structure where I wasn't the eldest anymore. I also became curious about how many more siblings I might have out there in the world. All of this significantly shifting my self-identity. It was around this age my stomach aches started. With what I know now, I believe I began to have deep feelings of unworthiness and unlovableness (not technically a word). The core human needs of certainty, safety and security had been shaken.

It wasn't until I was twenty-seven that I found out how many more siblings I had. It turns out he also made the next woman pregnant, the one he was cheating on my mum with. I am therefore one of six children to him, between four different women. I have learned since then, how people can make meaning about how they see themselves when it comes to their place in the family. A change in the family structure and where we feel we belong in it, can absolutely influence our self-perception and self-esteem. Not always for everyone but for me, it did.

As you know from Chapter One, I did the internal work to resolve the feelings I had because of the absence of my biological father. I am so grateful to have had all the love and support of my family and friends around me. Thanks to their love and acceptance, I was able to find the path to process my feelings and get the help I needed. All of this was a catalyst for me to find my calling in personal development and the human potential movement. I am tremendously grateful for finding my path early in life. Discovering my desire to help others deepen their own self-awareness and help them realise their abilities to create their lives the way they want to, has been a great blessing for me.

Our relationship to our power

My story is no more significant, unique, or important than anyone else's. We all have our own story, which informs who we have become today. My story is not particularly unique when it comes to family structures and relationships.

My story is universal with our past experiences informing the beliefs we create about ourselves. We feel and behave as if they are true. Our pasts create our relationship to our power, until we empower ourselves. Up until the age of seven years old, we are like sponges, who learn about the world through what we see, hear, touch, taste, smell and feel.

We learn about what words to use in certain interactions with people. We learn hello, goodbye, thanks, yes and no. We learn to blow kisses at loved ones and say 'Bless you!' when someone sneezes. My fifteen-month-old daughter does that already; we pick these things up incredibly quickly!

Perhaps deeper than learning words or how to move our body, we are already starting to attribute meaning to events and relationships that set the foundation for the rest of our lives.

We are creating relationships and allocate meaning to;

- how we connect and relate to other people,
- our perceptions of our body,
- our place in the world,
- what it means to be loved and how to love,
- what is food and health,
- what to value as important in our world,
- what is money, and how it relates to daily life and it goes on and on.

We create many beliefs and perceptions before we turn seven years old. We are like little sponges simply absorbing the outside world, accepting our perceptions as true, until we experience something different which proves otherwise. Our meanings and beliefs are set, whether they work for us or not, resourceful or unresourceful. We only start to think about what is true for us, as a unique individual, when we begin to have the capacity to judge what is best for us and what is another person's belief and influence. As adults, with more choice and awareness, we discover there are many other possibilities that are true, too.

When we were children, we attributed meaning to everything in the world and how we fit into it, as if we were the centre of the universe. Children continually reference their experiences back to themselves. For example, if their parents are angry, it is common for the child to feel they have done something wrong. If a child doesn't get the attention they want, over time, they may create a belief they are not lovable.

A critical factor in how we make meaning is through who influences us the most whilst we are learning about the world during this pivotal period? For most people, this is our parents. For those who don't grow up with a parent, their primary guardian will have this place. Still, biological parents will have an impact on us because it is innate from birth to expect to feel loved by the people who created us.

We pick up many wonderful things from our parents if we had loving and caring parents, we all deserve. Thanks to them we were given life and opportunities to grow into the unique adult we are today. Most parents have loving intentions and did the best they could. Sadly, many people can also have parents who were not so positive in nature, and from this, learnt lessons and became who they did as they had to work on overcoming all the problems that brought. We can have parents who are either positive or negative in nature, a mix of either say if one parent was loving and the other abusive. Regardless of how we were parented, any influence is worthwhile exploring simply because we are separate adults to them, living in a different environment to what they did. We are not saying that all parents are negative because we are influenced by them. We do say that there will always be some negativity of the influence though because **no matter what our parents' intentions were or how they behaved, we can create perceptions from our childhood that are negative for us to hold on to.** Please understand the difference.

Exploring our parental influence is key when it comes to unlocking our potential. If we don't evaluate, clear and create our own beliefs about the world as independent adults, we will just relive the limitations of our parents. They adopted their behaviours and perceptions from their parents, who gained it from theirs… and you get the picture. People adopt meaning according to how their parents did. It is the nature of learning, living, and evolving.

As a parent myself, I understand how confronting this can be. We can either choose to repeat the patterns from the past, which come from decades of meaning from entirely different environments and eras. Including going through wars and the depression. Yes, we have some significant world events and wars now, (plus a certain pandemic) and for most of us who will be reading this, it is still a different environment because of the advancements we have today. It is my white privilege acknowledging that I have not had to experience any type of war and I am sorry for anyone reading this who is or has.

We either self-reflect, learn, make change, and evolve with the new environment and time. Or we simply repeat the patterns of our parents and ancestors. This is not about blaming our parents or guardians for how we turned out; it is just understanding what we've learned about this world from the people who made us and were there (or not there) teaching us about the world. It is entirely about taking responsibility for challenging those thoughts and behaviours we do automatically without questioning what doesn't work for us today. It is simply appreciating how we learn as human beings.

I had a student in an NLP training recently tell me she had never spoken up if she had a differing opinion to her husband. She was afraid of arguing in front of her three children and impacting them negatively. She then went on to say, upon reflection, she wished she had been open, honest and spoken up, no matter the reaction from her husband. She feels by not speaking up and being afraid to have negative energy in the household, she might have shown her children that it isn't okay to have a differing opinion. Also, she didn't show them an example of being able to speak up that is empowering and healthy for everyone. In wanting to be mindful in one way, we could be disempowering in another.

We might as well be honest with ourselves and show up authentically and with all our imperfections to see what comes from that instead. This incredible woman now chooses to be her true self in front of her children so she can teach them the importance of speaking up. This is the thing with being parents; we do our best, and we can't be in control of the meaning our children will make. So, we might as well just be ourselves.

Have you challenged your beliefs as an adult? I find it interesting how many people can live their entire lives without stopping to really question their beliefs, the meaning they have assigned to things and consequently, the relationships they have created in all areas of their lives. A large part of my role as a coach is to be there for people when they start to evaluate their unconscious beliefs. I then give them practical and immediate guidance on helping them change any unresourceful ones. We all have the potential inside us to make profound and lasting change, no matter how long we have held onto something that hasn't served us.

Anxiety tells us when we feel powerless

All the small things we continue to allow in our lives which are not good for us, yet we don't change by taking action, tend to wear on our energy levels. We let go of our power each time we fall victim to our own negative choices.

I was inspired to write this after a client came to see me because she hadn't been happy in her workplace for a long time. Not because she doesn't love what she does and the contribution she makes. Rather because of the impact of the environment and people around her. She feels bullied, belittled and unappreciated. She came to me with so much anxiety. We uncovered how she came to be at this point simply because she fundamentally felt in the circumstances, she had lost her power.

Anxiety creates more anxiety. The more we worry about things not working out in the future, the more we program our mind to want to problem-solve all our made-up future problems. It's a protection mechanism to help us feel in control, when really, we just feel powerless and stuck. Anxiety is not having a sense of control; when we don't feel in control, we lose our sense of power. Then we forget where our place of power is. It is only ever in the present moment.

We like to project ourselves into the future in our mind's eye to feel a sense of control over our future, to feel safe. It's like we program ourselves to think that if we can solve all of our future problems now, we can feel secure. And life doesn't work like this. We can only do something in the present moment because it is the only place we can take action.

Let's look at how we can practice being in our place of power, the present moment, for each area of our life.

Holding our power in each area of our lives

When it comes to power, it is essential to understand this secret and crucial key to self-love, having discernment. The English Collins Dictionary defines discernment as "the ability to judge which things of a particular kind are good and which are bad."

Discernment is similar to the word *decision* because we choose one idea over another. Life continually asks us to make decisions, and it is crucial for our wellbeing and happiness that we make the most self-loving decisions.

Many women need to understand, the most self-loving decision for themselves is always the most loving for others too. This point is one I usually need to say twice if I am sharing this with someone. It's not an easy point to hit home the first time we hear it. Yet it is vital for us to grasp, so it bears repeating.

Think about it: if someone is doing something for you with resentment, would you want them to feel this way about it? High chance you don't. People-pleasing which is not self-loving is superficial. Since you are acting one way but feeling like you wish you weren't. It eats you up inside. How does it show love for another person if we attempt to make them happy to the detriment of our own happiness? It doesn't. The people you love want you to be happy, too. *If they don't, spend your energy on those who do.* This isn't always easy. It doesn't serve the greater good when we suffer for the sake of others. A context where there is exception is when you are a parent to young children as they literally depend on you for their survival.

I hear you asking, 'But Lauren, what about when I make a self-loving decision that will undeniably hurt the person, such as breaking up with them and breaking their heart? How can this decision be most loving to them?' Well, here is the point to add: if it doesn't appear to be loving in the short term, as people can feel hurt, it's likely to be loving in the long term. Who would ever want to be with someone because they pitied you or because they are afraid to hurt your feelings? No one. Everyone wants to be deeply and truly loved. In this situation, breaking up with them to go and find someone who will love them, even if they feel heartbroken at first, is a decision coming from love.

So, the most self-loving decision you make for yourself in any situation is always the most loving for others. Self-love considers all consequences, genuinely cares about the feelings and wellbeing of others, and prioritises the highest good of all involved. Sometimes it can mean people are disappointed in the short term, but when coming from this place of genuine love, it is the best decision long term.

Do you need to make more self-loving decisions than you have in the past?

We can break down each area of our lives into categories. One of the best ways we can do this is to go over the chakras we learned in chapter two. We want to reflect on each area of our lives and give a scale out of ten for our self-love.

I have the Self-Love Principle for each chakra below. I want you to ask your unconscious mind for a number out of ten where a ranking of one is you need to have a lot of improvement in this area. Ten is you couldn't get any better right now. It's incredibly true for you, and no action needs to be taken in the short term.

Here we go.

1. *Do I love myself enough to be grounded in my body and do I respect my relationship with the physical realm? eg. my health, finances and environments like home and office? Have I created a space in my life where I feel like I belong?*
My rating today out of ten is: _____
2. *Do I love myself enough to master my emotions and enjoy pleasure?*
My rating today out of ten is: _____
3. *Do I love myself enough to look after my boundaries and stand up for what is important to me?*
My rating today out of ten is: _____
4. *Do I love myself enough to have loving relationships with loving connection to myself and others?*
My rating today out of ten is: _____
5. *Do I love myself enough to communicate my needs, wants and*

speak up for what is important to me?
My rating today out of ten is: _____
6. *Do I love myself enough to listen and follow my intuition?*
My rating today out of ten is: _____
7. *Do I love myself enough to feel at one with all, and have a deep connection to something bigger than myself?*
My rating today out of ten is: _____

After this reflection it's good to take time to think about what discerning decisions we need to make in each area of our life. In other words:

- **What do we need to stop, let go of and say no to? and**
- **What do we want to keep, do more, and say big yeses to?**

Before we move on to the next exercise, we need to understand if we are living our lives for others, from the influence of others or for ourselves from our own power and influence?

Are we living our lives for others, from the influence of others or for ourselves?

In Matrix Therapies®, created by Pip McKay, there is a section called *The Archetypal Stages of Growth*. It is a profound model which helps us learn to stop holding ourselves back and instead get the results we want in each area of our lives. I will briefly describe here. It has many complex layers, however I'll explain what we need to know to make progress on the next exercise in this chapter. We go into a deeper explanation in our training.

The Archetypal Stages of Growth by Pip McKay

The Archetypal Stages of Growth model explains four stages of growth;

1. Child
2. Teenager
3. Young Adult
4. Mature Adult.

We all grow up through these stages physically, with each having positive and negative traits. The positives in the child stage for example, are to feel free and have fun. The negative is to depend on others for survival. At a physical level, these stages are what we go through as we learn and experience life. When we understand our progression through these stages mentally, emotionally, and even spiritually, it gives us helpful insight into reaching more of our potential. The more we reach Mature Adult with our emotional intelligence, the more we have resourceful behaviours. This allows us to fulfil our potential and deepens our connections with others.

Let's look at the area of finances as an example and go through the Archetypal Stages of Growth. Someone who is frivolous, irresponsible and can't even face the fact there are bills to pay, is behaving like a child with money. Adults who can't look after themselves financially are in the Child stage. They want to escape the reality of how much things cost, escape paying bills and taxes and create ways to stay disillusioned about their financial position and money behaviours.

Someone who rebels against what they know is best for them and continues to sabotage making and keeping money is in Teenager. They may save but then mindlessly spend or rack up debt.

Someone who is independent financially but only wants to spend on themselves and can't be responsible for a family is stuck in the Young Adult stage. It is different if it's agreed that one parent stays home to look after young children and doesn't earn money in that time.

Whilst someone with resourceful money habits who continues to grow and learn about how to invest and create wealth, is a Mature Adult with money. They are also personally responsible for their money and can look after their family responsibilities.

There was a time in my adult life when I worked but continued to rely on my partner to save the money for our house deposit. I wouldn't save at all. I was also in denial about how much things cost and how much money I needed to earn to pay my way for things. If I wanted to go overseas, I would use a bank loan to do so and pay it off over years. I was in the Child and Teenager stages with money. Thankfully I learned about these growth stages and realised I wanted to be a Mature Adult and fulfil my financial potential. I 'grew up' in the area of money by becoming entirely responsible for earning what I needed, paying for expenses and taxes, saving and investing money for the financial wellbeing of myself and my future family.

We can apply these stages to any area of life. We go through them in depth at Evolve Now! Level 1B: Masculine & Feminine Coaching workshop, where we elaborate about the different behaviours in each stage. It is life-changing to learn how to get more of what we want in life and be truly self-responsible Mature Adults in every area.

The Archetypal Stages of Growth by Pip McKay, in relation to influence and our personal power

We are often entirely unaware of how much others influence us. So it is helpful to use a process that engages the unconscious mind to let go of these influences. As discussed, if we continue to be influenced negatively by others, we lose our power because we repeat the patterns of the past which no longer serve us. In our training, Evolve Now! Level 1C: Matrix Therapies®, we clear parental programming and other key people of influence. To discover more about why it is transformational to clear parental programming, learning Archetypal Stages of Growth by Pip McKay, is incredibly profound. Let's go over the model again in relation to parental programming and the shadow (negative) aspects of each stage of influence;

1. Child - adopts
2. Teenager - rebels
3. Young Adult - escapes
4. Mature Adult – compensates

Child

For each area of life, we could be adopting, (which means to take them on as our own) beliefs, emotions, and behaviours from those who have influenced us (such as parents or guardians). Adopting is in the Child stage. Children take on the world like sponges, particularly up to the age of seven. Absorbing the world according to how the adults in their lives did. What meaning did our parents give to handling emotions and communication? What meaning did our parents give to the way they eat? The list goes on. Another example is around money; we could be adopting from a parent the stress and workaholic behaviours they had to earn money.

When we were children, we generally looked to our guardians to give us permission about trusting another adult or not. This is useful as a child to ensure of safety when we are vulnerable. If we don't learn as adults that it is up to us to create our own barometer of safety, we can walk around in life waiting for others to give us permission about being accepted and safe. We tend to put the term "shyness" to this structure, Pip McKay says 'shyness is waiting for someone else to let us know we can be ourselves'. This is giving our power away to others. Instead, we want to confidently parent ourselves. To know we can be safe and have permission to trust others by using our own intuition and judgement.

As mentioned before, children are self-referential, which means they feel the external world reflects something they have done or because of who they are. This means when they see their parents argue, they think it is about them or their fault. Or they think others might not want to play with them because there must be something wrong with them. They don't have the capacity to realise the other children are just not aware of them. If we still have this belief as adults, it's another form of giving away our power.

Instead, we want to parent ourselves to know the world doesn't revolve around us and we have more choice as an adult than ever before. We have choices on how we interpret events, process them, communicate and act effectively.

Teenager

In any area of life, we could be experiencing results because we are rebelling against the beliefs, emotions, and behaviours of those who influenced us. Rebelling is part of the Teenager stage of growth. An example of rebelling is if a person was brought up having to save money and never be able to spend it. This could create a rebellion as an adult of not saving at all. Or for someone else, it could be their parents always spent excessively, so they could become a miser and they don't even spend money on necessary things. Rebelling meant they became scared of spending money.

An example of rebelling in health, is if someone was raised never to eat junk food. When they grow older and can choose what they eat, they may overeat junk food, even if it doesn't make them feel good (which is most likely). It's become out of balance for them because they want the feeling of freedom and independence. This is the nature of emotional logic. Even though it doesn't consciously make sense to the person to have these behaviours, the emotions are driving them to act in this way because of the past influence of others. Rather than from what is best for them now. Eating junk food means freedom and independence at the emotional level for them. While logically, eating the food makes them feel sick and doesn't really make them happy, which they are striving to feel fundamentally. Once the influence is realised that they don't have to rebel with food (or anything else) to feel freedom and independence. Then they can more easily find healthier ways to feel freedom and independence.

Teenagers go from being self-referential as a child to a more external reference. They look to peers and role models outside of the family structure to see what is socially acceptable. It can mean they hide parts of themselves, if they feel ashamed for how they learned behaviours as a child. They may fear they won't be accepted by those around them, particularly friends. A teenager in the shadow thinks things like 'No one understands me or my ideas.' They feel that *no one gets me*.

Whereas a child's core negative feeling would be things like unsupported, unloved, unsafe, sad, and afraid. These are repressive emotions because when we feel them, we don't want to do anything. We are passive in response. We are a victim of our circumstances.

A teenager's, core negative emotions are anger, rage, frustration, even arrogance. We experience these emotions when we find ourselves rebelling against what people say. If we often think, 'Go away!' Or using profanities or shouting, 'Don't tell me what to do!' Then it is likely a teenager part of us wanting to protect an unresolved inner child.

How we commonly feel in a certain area of life, can illuminate what stage of growth we are currently at. Let's reflect for a moment; when it comes to how you feel about yourself, do you feel more repressed. Do you have childlike emotions such as sadness and lack of confidence in who you are? Or do you hold a lot of anger and strive for independence with a strong feeling of not being told what to do? Do you feel that you've more child or teenager going on inside of you? You could perhaps have both. Perhaps you've really moved through both stages and are at the Young Adult stage of self-esteem.

At Young Adult stage, we are clear about who we are and are more self-reliant for approval. This is because we have matured by processing the child and teenager emotions. We have realised, 'You know what? I know myself now. I know what's important to me and am willing to take full responsibility for myself and my life.'

Young Adult
At this stage, a person is fully responsible for themselves but doesn't want to be responsible for others. This can prevent them from having a family or fully committing to a long term relationship. If they feel they can't avoid a responsibility they don't want or if someone puts pressure on them in any way, they are likely to choose to escape.

The Young Adult stage is not dependent on anyone like a child would be nor do they need to rebel like a teenager because they don't have to be at home. People at this stage don't feel they can maintain their independence in the face of other's needs. They are afraid they may become co-dependant like a child, or rebellious like a teenager and they don't want to feel that form of powerlessness or confrontation. So, they simply leave these situations. They feel 'I'm better off on my own, then I don't need to deal with this shit', particularly when things are hard. This makes long term relationships difficult because they don't like to feel vulnerable or have difficult conversations. When they can do this, they grow to Mature Adult stage in this context.

If there are unresolved issues between key influential people, escaping means escaping their influence, like moving country or as far away as possible. The core negative emotions of the young adult are of feeling lost and wanting to escape. If things are too hard, they want to avoid it at almost all costs. It can feel lonely with scattered thoughts of 'What should I do next? And what's really my truth?' To become a Mature Adult, they need to learn to be themselves at the same time as engaging with others.

We know we are not influenced by others when we don't need to adopt, rebel or escape. If we notice we compensate, this is coming from influence too.

Mature Adult
The final way we can behave influenced by others is by compensation. This is the shadow of being in the Mature Adult stage of growth. Examples of this could be if someone had parents who were misers with money, then they may compensate by being overly generous or exorbitant with spending money on others. Or if someone didn't get their parents' love, nurture and attention, compensation could turn into wanting to rescue others even when they don't ask for help. This person might overly indulge in people-pleasing behaviour because underneath are beliefs that if they give love and save others, they will be loved back. For someone else, compensation could turn into building an empire on more material, external things to feel happy. They will eventually realise their happiness comes from within and nothing externally will make them feel more loved and fulfilled without doing the inner work of giving love and nurture to their unresolved inner children.

This stage in the light allows us to take full responsibility for ourselves and be appropriately responsible for others. The Mature Adult can balance their own needs in the face of other's needs. Create boundaries when needed but at the same time can relate to others with compassion and empathy. They can love themselves at the same time as loving others and find win/

win solutions to conflict rather than sacrificing themselves.

These are all the shadow aspects of how others influence us and why it is helpful to let go of the influence of parental programming, of other people or even groups of people. Each stage has the light (positive) aspect, too, and the way we reach our greatest potential is to do as much of the light as possible. To grow up on all levels and become Mature Adults in each area of our life, a Matrix Therapies® Master Practitioner can take you through the process, or at one of our Evolve Now or NLP Training courses. When we let go of negative influences, it can bring us closer to the people whose influence we clear (if we want to) or they are naturally and easily let go of if needed. It allows us to make decisions which are the best and most loving for all involved.

I have created this exercise below which encompasses all the information from this chapter to reclaim our power. To live in our highest potential, we need to continually practice discernment in each area of our lives. Please note, if you don't find it easy to do the upcoming exercise, it may be worth working with a Matrix Therapies® Master Practitioner to help you clear negative influences in your life first.

Practice being in our place of power, the present moment, for each area of our life

Remember, we only have power in the present moment. Each moment of our lives, we can make a choice to choose differently and more wisely through what we learn. Today, take stock of each area of your life and notice, what is best for you - and consequently others. What is best to stop doing, cut away and say 'no' to? Then, thinking about what you want to keep allowing, giving permission to, accepting and inviting into your life by saying 'yes' to.

I also have the following questions in the journal and online workbook at www.laurenjobson.com/bookfreecourse, if you would like to participate there. I have my free self-love planner at www.lovelifewithlauren.com.au. It gives you daily prompts that help you be more discerning in your life.

A beautiful exercise to do to enhance the experience of answering the questions below is **to put one hand to your heart, then breathing into that, with your eyes closed, say:**

'When I love myself,
when I respect myself,
I know in my heart, I am a good person,
with the best intentions for me and for everybody.
What is good for me to cut away, and what is good for me to keep?'

1. In the area of my spiritual life and what this means to me. What do I want to stop? What do I want to keep doing?

I say no to:
_____
_____

I say yes to:
_____
_____

2. In the area of my mental life and what this means to me, such as education, learning, and mental stimulation. What would I like to stop? What would I like to do more of?

I say no to:

_____
_____

I say yes to:

_____
_____

3. In my work life and what this means to me. What would I like to do less of or stop altogether? What would I like to keep doing?

I say no to:

_____
_____

I say yes to:

_____
_____

4. In the area of my love life and what this means to me, such as family, friends, and connection to everyone in my life. Who or what do I need to let go of or have more boundaries with? What and who would I like to invite into my life?

I say no to:

_____
_____

I say yes to:

_____
_____

5. In the area of my wealth and what this means to me. What do I need to do less of and say no to? What do I need to do more of and say yes to?

I say no to:

_____
_____

I say yes to:

_____
_____

6. In the area of my social life and what this means to me. What do I need to say no to? What do I say yes to?

I say no to:

_____
_____

I say yes to:

_____
_____

7. In the area of my physical life and what this means to me, such as my health, wellbeing, and environment. What do I need to stop doing? What do I need to keep doing?

I say no to:

_____

_____

I say yes to:

_____

_____

Conclusion of this vow

I vow to make self-loving decisions.
I honour the relationship I have with my power.

Discernment truly is the crucial key to loving ourselves. It is a continual journey of deciding what is best for us and taking action in the most loving and resourceful ways.

When it comes to discernment, your unconscious mind wants you to let go of any limiting beliefs about yourself, doubts, and blocks. It wants you to be more positive, have more compassion, and positivity in your self-talk. It will do anything to help guide you to feel happier, healthier, more joyful and have more gratitude for your beautiful life. Cut away all the stuff that doesn't serve you. You deserve to love who you are because it doesn't help anyone else not to. **Plus making self-loving decisions are always most loving for others too.**

A summary of what you learned in Chapter Four

I Vow to Make Self-Loving Decisions.
I honour the relationship I have with my power.

- Lauren's story on growing up the oldest of three, and relationship to her power
- Our relationship to our power
- Anxiety tells us when we feel powerless
- Holding our power in each area of our lives
- The Archetypal Stages of Growth by Pip McKay
- The Archetypal Stages of Growth when it comes to influence and our personal power
- Practice being in our place of power, the present moment, for each area of our life

Devoting yourself to applying the learnings in this chapter:

1. Using the Self-Loving Resources of Tools and Mindset: Grab your journal or my workbook I created for you at www.laurenjobson.com/bookfreecourse

Ask yourself these powerful questions below. Go within to listen to what answers come to you and write them down without judgement or questioning. No one else needs to see your answers so go ahead and deepen your connection to the relationship you have with your own power and unconscious mind.

Q1. Do I love myself enough to stand up to what is important to me even when my path is not easy? How can I do so, more often? (This question relates to being in the Child stage of growth).

Q2. Do I wait for permission from others to make me feel safe and accepted?

If so, to who and how? How can I parent myself to feel confident and safe around others? (This question also relates to being in the Child stage of growth.)

Q3. Do I rebel when it's not necessary and find myself being reactive? (This question relates to being in the Teenager stage of growth.)

Q4. Do I sway from my truth or feel any shame, so I hide those parts of myself to fit in and be accepted?

If so, with who and what do I hide? (This question also relates to being in the Teenager stage of growth.)

Q5. Do I escape when I need to make commitments?

If so, what am I afraid of and how can I parent myself to grow up and face it? (This question relates to being in the Young Adult stage of growth.)

Q6. Is my need for freedom at all costs becoming destructive or stopping me making long term goals? (This question also relates to being in the Young Adult stage of growth.)

Q7. Do I compensate in any area of my life? Am I doing too much for others or rescuing them? (This question relates to the Mature Adult stage of growth.)

Q8. Am I bored with my life and feel so secure that I feel I need something new? (This question also relates to the Mature Adult stage of growth.)

2. Using the Self-Loving Resource of Support: A Matrix Therapies® Master Practitioner or coach can help you form and listen to your own words and feed back what they are hearing. This helps you know what decisions to make next. They can also help you clear negative influences, particularly parental programming, regardless of how they were as parents. In our 1 to 1 coaching sessions, we clear both the influence of mum and dad since they were the main masculine and feminine role models in our lives. In doing so, we can connect with the resources of masculine and feminine energies discussed in Chapter One.

3. Using the Self-Loving Resource of Intuition: This is our wise, calm inner voice. It is our gut and body wisdom, our inner mentor to trust and follow. We all need to learn how to listen to our intuition more often and deepen our relationship with this inner wise one. Our intuition is our most profound and most trustworthy resource. We learn how to connect with it in Chapter Seven.

4. Using the Self-Loving Resource of Forgiveness: This is a reminder that life and self-love is a process. Do what you feel drawn to and practise forgiveness. Particularly self-forgiveness. I also like EFT (emotional freedom technique) for forgiveness as the script is beautiful: "Even though I (state problem), I deeply and completely, love and accept myself". I will share resources on how to do this in my online course at www.laurenjobson.com/bookfreecourse. Again, doing Matrix Therapies® is also wonderful for the practise of forgiveness.

Chapter Five

I Vow to Talk to Myself with Perspective, Compassion & Forgiveness.

I honour the relationship I have with my judgements and inner voice.

Vow Five

"If only we talked to ourselves like we do to our besties, we would fulfil so much more of our potential."

LAUREN JOBSON

Sometimes there are stories we tell ourselves so often they become ingrained in our self-perception. We don't even realise they are a story simply made up in our mind. These thoughts become our self-identity. It's only when we become self-aware enough to see them clearly we realise how false and detrimental they have been.

It might be a surprise for some of those who know me to learn, one such story that has played on repeat in my unconscious mind. It's how inadequate I feel around other women. It's not apparent on the surface of my behaviours. My earliest memory of this story was when I was in my last year of primary school and thinking about who I would meet when I went to high school. Whenever I heard something about a student who would be in my class, it didn't take long for me to create a story in my mind of how "cool" they were compared to me. I would feel particularly inadequate around those I perceived to be confident, self-assured, and beautiful. It seems I forgot to think those things about myself too.

I can honestly say for most of my high school years, I felt intimated, *less than,* and self-critical around those I would perceive as better than me. It's funny because I took on leadership roles where I was confident in certain aspects. I can appreciate the irony as others probably felt I was highly confident and self-assured. Yet, truly on the inside, my feelings and self-talk were playing a conflicting story.

As I write this book at the age of 35, it is only now I am unravelling this story and how it has shown up with those closest to me, particularly those who have strong feminine roles in my life. In resolving and working through some conflicts and built up energy between us, I finally understand the power of my unconscious beliefs with how they have affected my ability to fully express myself as I would have liked to and how I have felt.

The unconscious belief that I feel less than, not good enough and inadequate around certain people, has meant I perceived things in our relationships a certain way. This is quite different from how the other person perceived me. An example is my fear of doing something the other person would perceive as "wrong" or hurtful. This causes me not to be myself at certain times and to question myself constantly. It's been hugely tiring and limiting! I am so glad to be breaking through this old and deep pattern. Thanks to those who have held the space for me to work through conflict and miscommunication at times and allowed me to see the false story for what it was.

When we can see through our stories, we can let them go and have a completely different experience in our relationships, thoughts, feelings, self-talk and behaviours. When we perceive ourselves differently, our world rearranges itself according to our new perception. Relationships deepen, the true us is seen and heard, and a new level of freedom and beauty enters our experiences.

When I left the music industry, I did not build up a big story about why I couldn't just quit my job, even when I had no idea what I would do next. Instead, I felt my emotions of not wanting to be there. I was so unhappy and being there was in conflict with what my heart wanted for me. I didn't have any huge commitments or responsibilities at that time in my life, so I could act resourcefully by listening to what my feelings were telling me, trusting my intuition, and simply telling my boss I was resigning. As you know, I did.

I was still wondering what I would do with my life after leaving the music industry. I felt I would just know what my next step would be once I had quit my job. I felt it would just fall into place and appear to me. Easier said than done, right? There were days of excitement with the adventure of the unknown, yet there were many moments of fearing things would not work out. And when I was in this state of fear, I was telling myself stories.

Stories such as, 'What if there is no better next step? What if I can't find a job I love? Is it even possible to find my passion for something else, now that my "dream job" hadn't been my dream after all? Could I dream again?'

It had been a few weeks of looking for jobs online. I was starting to feel lost and a little hopeless about the possibility I would just have to settle for something I didn't have any passion for. This was a soul-crushing thought for me. I felt I had a big calling. I knew it. I just couldn't see it yet, which was very confusing.

One day, my Uncle Simon (the same uncle who referred me to see the therapist who helped me overcome my stomach pains) invited me over to his place to help him in his business for the day. I had a good idea of his business since I had experienced one of his weekend workshops that changed my life around intimate relationships (a story for Chapter Eight). I also graduated his NLP Practitioner Training while studying for the music industry.

It turned out to be a pivotal moment in my life; of course, I didn't know it yet. I wasn't sitting down at the big wooden dining table for too long before he asked me, 'Lauren, whilst you are looking for another job, would you like to work for me in my business and help me out a few days a week?'

It was like a bigger part of me knew I had to do it. The "yes" flew out of my mouth before I had time to think. I could feel the excitement bubbling up in me.

I never felt I had to find my calling ever again. But I did have to do all sorts of things that weren't aligned with my heart before I could make my dream my full-time career. This was mostly due to my own limitations. My next step had appeared to me. This experience of working with him fifteen years ago became my foundational platform that catapulted me to where I am today. I'm now a leader in the field of NLP in Australia. I have my own Human Potential Personal Development Coaching and Training company; Intuitive Heart Training Academy.

Today I spend my time teaching and guiding people in how to deeply understand and heal past stuck emotions so they can improve their lives and relationships.

Our relationship to our thinking - our stories are not who we are

I love the concept of our self-talk simply being stories we tell ourselves. Immediately when we hear this, we can be reminded those thoughts we feel to be real are just made up in our head. We are the creator of the movies inside our minds. Indeed, we can change them whenever we decide to.

We are both the thinker and the observer at the same time. As you read this, you can, at the very same time, make judgements of what you are reading and observe yourself as the reader.

We have to be more than our observations because we can act, think, talk, and process our external world while simultaneously observing and judging ourselves doing so. This then tells us we must be more than our thoughts, behaviours, and the inner voice we all know too well.

This concept can be a sigh of relief for us. Since we are separate from the observer, we can change how we observe and make meaning in this world and the perceptions we make about ourselves. So how do you perceive yourself? How do you observe your thoughts and actions?

The stories we play in our minds, which feel so personal and true to us can dictate how we experience so much of our lives. Stories such as:

- ♥ I am not good enough to have a loving partner who accepts me for who I am because (insert experience here such as biological father abandoned me. Therefore, men leave me), so there must be something wrong with me.

- I am not worthy of having a successful business because who am I to make more money than my friends and family by simply doing what I love?
- It is unsafe to play life at a bigger level because I will only be criticised and judged by others.

This list could go on because we all have stories we tell ourselves from all we have experienced up until now. What is a story you tell yourself that feels true yet disempowers you and is not self-loving?

How is our self-talk created?

Let's look again for a moment at how a human being processes information. We can see how our self-talk is created and what it does for us in terms of creating our behaviours.

The NLP Communication Model

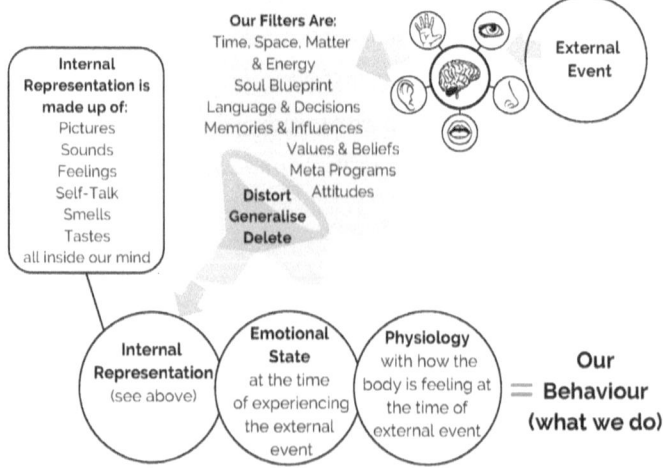

Firstly, we process an external event from our outside world through our five senses. We see, touch, hear, taste and smell, and in a split second, we filter this information through our memories, values, beliefs, attitudes and personality traits. Once our unconscious mind has deleted, distorted and generalised information according to these filters, we create an experience inside our mind that includes internal pictures, sounds, feelings, smells and tastes and the big one we are most familiar with consciously, our self-talk.

The internal representation we have in our conscious mind is what creates our focus. It determines the meaning we assign to an experience. Self-talk, amongst the pictures/movies, feelings, sounds, smells and tastes in your mind, equals what you focus on and the meaning you put to an event. Coupled at the same time as your emotional state, plus the way your body was feeling, creates how you feel about yourself and the actions you then take.

Self-talk is generally the outcome of our filters. When we change our beliefs, values, emotions about our past, our perception of memories and so on we can more easily change our self-talk. It will organically change. My story of inadequacy was fuelled by my beliefs and perceptions I had made from my past. Believing I am just as worthy, amazing, and loved as other people, has changed my self-talk and my life.

If we want better thoughts, we must learn to ask ourselves better questions. If we wish to find more solutions and be more resourceful, we will need to ask ourselves better questions. Our unconscious mind simply receives the question and answers it accordingly. For example, if you are saying to yourself (or out loud!), 'Why is this so hard?' your unconscious mind will search for reasons for it to be hard and validate that suggestion from the very nature of the question. If we ask instead, 'How could this be easier?' imagine the different answers our unconscious mind will receive and inform us of. We use negative language too often as we are creating a focus on what we don't want instead of what we do. 'How can I find a solution?' is a great thought to have instead of focusing on the problem itself.

Let's look at how we create negative, non-self-loving thoughts in our minds, through the stories we tell ourselves.

There is nothing self-loving about believing our stories are true

The difference between someone with healthy self-love and one who needs to develop and grow theirs, is the person's level of attachment to their stories being true.

One simple way we can start to let go of negative self-talk is by stopping and reflecting on where our story has come from. When we can be aware of the story, we discover the meaning we are putting to our current experience. From this, we can learn and take the necessary action.

In the next chapter, we look at SEAing our emotions:

- ♥ S - stands for the **sensation** we feel in our body, most likely reacting to a **story** we are telling ourselves. We want to take the time here to stop, listen, reflect and then...
- ♥ E – **emote** and **evaluate** the story and where it comes from to...

- ♥ A – **accept** it, **acknowledge** and **allow** it, and take the **appropriate action**.

Why do our stories feel so real and true to us?

The experience of being strongly attached to our stories and thoughts feeling true occurs because they *were* real - once upon a time in our inner child's mind. At least, the meaning that was made there was real.

For example, if I have a story about making mistakes means I am not worthy enough to achieve what I want to and I have to be perfect. This most likely would have come from a time in childhood when that meaning was informed from an event in my life. An event when I may have made a mistake and was criticised in some way. Then my unconscious mind creates a belief about how not being perfect equals not being worthy of creating and achieving what I want. This is an example of how emotional logic works, which I will go over in the next chapter.

Children create many meanings about the world depending on what they experienced. They make all this meaning about what happens around them and believe it all has something to do with them. They are self-referential because their growing brains continuously determine what the world means to them and how they fit into it. This means children take everything personally.

For instance, I had underlying feelings of not feeling good enough because my biological father didn't love me enough to be the parent I wanted him to be. No one had to teach me what it meant to have a father. It is just something I innately expected. We are all born knowing we want love, nurture, safety, protection, to be seen, significant, and so on. Every human innately expects to be parented ideally, even when we don't consciously know what parents are. We don't need to be taught to expect these things; we just do. My inner child felt I wasn't worthy or good enough because of my biological father's choices.

The different kinds of untrue stories – cognitive distortions

Have you ever heard of having all-or-nothing thinking? What about overthinking or catastrophising? I had heard of some of these labels. Still, when I came across the research on "common cognitive distortions", it opened my mind to go gentler on myself. Knowing that what I was doing in my head was natural, even if unresourceful and uncomfortable.

In the 1970s, psychologist Aaron Beck proposed the theory of cognitive distortions. He noticed many of his patients who experienced depression relied on false assumptions and errors in thinking. He believed if his patients could change those inaccurate thoughts (cognitive distortions), they would be able to change their symptoms of depression.

Beck's student, Dr David Burns, continued the research on cognitive distortions and popularised the concept with his book, *Feeling Good: The New Mood Therapy*, in which he shared common examples of cognitive distortions. Dr David Burns also did a TED talk called *Feeling Good*, where he explained some great examples of distorted thinking and how he encouraged his clients to challenge those thoughts.

Here are some of the cognitive distortions we can become aware of inside our minds. In knowing these exist, I can catch myself more quickly, allowing me to observe myself gently and acknowledge the thoughts. Whilst knowing that this very likely is an untrue story I am telling myself. I have noticed my default distortions are; catastrophising, the fallacy of fairness, emotional reasoning, and personalisation. See which ones you tend to do more commonly from the list below.

They include:

- **Overthinking or overanalysing** where the stories get more complex with more and more mind-reads of what we think others might be thinking.
- **Jumping to conclusions or mind-reading**, such as needing to predict future outcomes and being convinced we know what others will do and are thinking.
- **All-or-nothing thinking or polarised thinking** where it is either one thing or the opposite with no middle ground. For example, 'I either get it perfect, or I don't do it at all.'
- **Catastrophising or exaggeration** is when we think of the worst-case scenario and magnify certain aspects of a situation. Also trying to solve all these made-up, magnified future problems in our mind.
- **Personalisation** is where we feel directly responsible for events which are out of our control and can quickly think we might have done something wrong when we haven't.
- **Filtering** removes and discounts the positives whilst focusing only on a situation's negatives.
- **Fallacy of change** is thinking others will meet our

expectations and needs if we pressure them enough.
- **Control fallacies** are when we believe we control others and situations entirely or feel we have no control over anything.
- **Fallacy of fairness** is feeling resentful when others don't measure fairness in the way we do and when we assume all things in life should be applied and measured based on fairness.
- **Overgeneralisation** is when we take an isolated event and turn it into a belief we will continue to experience, and it becomes a self-defeating pattern. For example, 'I am just not good at attracting the right partner.'
- **Blaming others** for how we feel and constantly feeling like the victim.
- **Always being right** causes us to feel we need to be correct. Being wrong is unacceptable, and one can go to great lengths to prove it.
- **Emotional reasoning** is seeing the situation through emotions, not facts.
- **Should Statements** are telling ourselves and others we should, shouldn't, or must do something with rigid rules, creating a lot of pressure on a situation. It can create guilt, frustration, even anger and resentment when disappointed by the outcome.
- **Labelling** is assigning labels to people based on an isolated event. Not considering the other behaviours of the person and discounting other times but immediately overgeneralising the person from one incident.

Aren't these helpful to know? We have all done some or all

of these at some point in our lives. Since coming across these terms, I can realise when my thoughts are just a distortion and reframe myself out of them. We can move through these thoughts, think about them much less often and recover from them. One way to do this is using Byron Katie's Four Questions, which I will share soon. But first, let's go over why we default to what is wrong with us, which would most closely be the distortions of personalisation, jumping to conclusions, catastrophising or even all-or-nothing thinking.

We default to what is wrong with us

I remember learning from Kelly McGonigal via the Udemy online course *The Neuroscience of Self Compassion* how she explained this concept regarding what we tend to do inside our minds. Kelly is a Stanford University psychologist, educator and author who brings science and stories together to help explain different human experiences.

It clicked for me from her teaching, how much our brain has a default position when we are not thinking about a specific task or concentrating on something in the present moment. We all have mind wandering, but did you know that our brain's default, whilst mind wandering, is to critique ourselves or others? To pick and focus on what is wrong with us? We default to think about the negative aspects of either;

- ♥ What we could have done better in the past
- ♥ The things we don't like about ourselves in the present or
- ♥ What could go wrong in a situation in the future?

Kelly explains this could be because we are a social species where our survival depends on being loved and belonging amongst other people. It's the core human need of love and connection. She describes rats' default brain position is to notice what they are smelling. Their survival depends on eating and knowing what they can eat next. If we need to belong and be loved, we must ensure our behaviours and qualities will support this. When we were hunters and gatherers, belonging in our tribe meant we would eat from the work of others we belonged to. That is why we do need to eat for our survival yet belonging has been most important to the human race.

It puts a whole new level to negative self-talk. We need to do better at putting conscious thought into setting our intentions with how we talk to ourselves. We want to direct our attention to self-loving thoughts and practices.

When our intention is to be kinder to ourselves, we can use this as our barometer for noticing our thoughts going off track from being self-loving. We then need to practise putting our attention to our intention to be conscious of whether our thoughts match our intent to be more self-loving. It's about creating new stories in our mind for how we want to act, feel, experience, and attract things into our life instead. I will go over how we do this after we learn "The Work".

I love Byron Katie's method to help with the practice of setting the intention for our thoughts to be as self-loving as possible. She created a process of self-examination by asking The Four Questions. Since it will be natural that we're not always loving with our thoughts, we want to become good at noticing when we think negatively about ourselves (and others). So we can change direction.

Byron Katie's "The Work" – Four Questions

In 2003, Byron Katie introduced the concept of "The Work" in her book *Loving What Is*. The story goes, in her early thirties Katie was so depressed and stuck in self-loathing that she was often unable to get out of bed for days or weeks at a time. She had the following recurring thoughts circling her mind such as 'my life is horrible,' and 'I don't deserve happiness.' Byron shares how one morning, in a sudden moment of life-changing insight, she saw her suffering came from her thoughts about her situation and not from the situation itself. She realised a simple truth. When she believed her thoughts, she suffered, and when she didn't, she was happy.

As I have explained earlier, we know that we think the way we do because of our past experiences. Our mind constantly refers to the past when faced with similar events because it feels it is doing the best for us by trying to keep us safe. When something feels familiar to the human brain, it feels safer, even when it is detrimental and unhealthy.

Out of this insight for Byron, she developed a process of self-inquiry which she now calls "The Work." It involves asking four simple questions about each belief or thought that causes us pain:

1. Is it true?
2. Can you absolutely know that it's true?
3. How do you react when you believe that thought?
4. Who would you be without the thought?

What these simple questions do is detach you from

heightened emotion. When I do it just by running a thought through these questions, I tend to sigh and relax my shoulders because I am now focused on who I could be without the thought. And I could choose to be that, right now.

"The Work" is commonly applied with judgements and emotional responses we have with others. After answering these questions, we are asked to come up with a turnaround sentence expressing the opposite of that thought or belief.

One easy way to begin learning how to do it is to access Katie's website (https://thework.com/en), where you'll find a detailed description.

How do we speak lovingly to ourselves? - Talk to yourself like a loving parent or best friend

The work of self-love is dedicating ourselves to becoming more conscious, more aware of our thoughts, the stories we play in our minds, our emotions and our choices going forward.

How do we speak lovingly to ourselves? The simple answer to this is to be our own parents. Since our emotions generally come from younger parts of ourselves stuck in painful times, we have stories we tell ourselves from this experience on repeat. We need to parent ourselves out of the situation by realising we are now adults with many more choices, resources, agency and wisdom than we had back then.

A trick I have picked up whilst having healthy self-love is noticing how I observe myself. Realising that now, this is how I would parent my actual biological child too. It's the qualities I put into my self-talk. Suppose I talk to myself like I would to a best friend or a beloved child; I naturally find I use a particular tone of voice that goes along with what I say. I have recorded examples you can hear if you go to www.laurenjobson.com/bookfreecourse to access these. By the tone of voice, I mean to talk more endearingly. I use a warm, low tone that shares compassion, respect, and genuine care.

I also notice the words I use to describe myself and use for judgments. Since we will make a judgement anyway; this is an idea of how to soften them. Saying, 'Oh, that was cute of you, Lauren,' particularly when my ego has been embarrassed in public. It immediately separates me from the behaviour I am observing because I can observe, judge, and then decide to talk to myself with grace. Just as I would towards another person I love and care for.

Instead of staying embarrassed and building on the implications that the humiliation would cause me to judge myself harshly, I use tone, words and saying my name kindly to change up this experience. Another example of what I could say would be: 'Oh, that's okay, Lauren; you did your best, and that was funny, wasn't it? How sweet or cute of you that your ego felt she wanted to do that,' and it helps me to move on. I see it for what it is; it was just a moment in time, and I know I can do better next time. It leads us to forgiveness and frees us up to give something another go. Regardless of how it made us feel the first time.

And yes, I do say my name, Lauren, when talking to myself, as it kindly acknowledges the fact that I am separate from my thoughts, observations, and behaviours. It is a disassociation technique, so as long as we take personal responsibility for our actions, it can be a healthy thing to do with our self-judgements.

Forgiveness is for you

As I mentioned in the introduction of this book and it bears repeating. In most instances, we need to be forgiving ourselves continually. For the things we wanted to do and didn't. For the things we felt we could have done better, but we didn't. Finding ourselves in certain situations we shouldn't have been in but were. For behaving, reacting, or interacting with another human being in a way that was not the most loving. We need to forgive ourselves for it all. Love can't shine through as wholly as it needs to when there is a block in the energy that is guilt, shame, regret, anger, resentment, or any other emotion that depletes our happiness.

To forgive is to listen to the lesson, take the learning on board and move forward. Sometimes moving on will be forgiving the other person involved, and sometimes it won't, which is okay. Let the person go compassionately and as resourcefully as possible or make sure to stand up for any new boundaries that need to come into play. If that is most self-loving to you. Then be in complete peace about it inside yourself.

All of us have things we wish we had done better and perhaps had times we cringe over when we think of how we behaved. We all have these times. We will very likely have more. Live, learn and be gentle with yourself. You are a human having a learning experience that is life. Since we all have these times and places to forgive ourselves, we might as well choose to do whatever it takes inside of us and through action, to allow ourselves to move on completely.

How else do we speak lovingly to ourselves? – Create new empowering stories

As mentioned earlier in this chapter, when we default to what is wrong with us to feel safe, we must learn to put intention into our lives. It starts with our thoughts to rewrite who and how we want to be. Suppose we don't set intentions to improve how we talk and perceive ourselves? How will we ever expect anything different in our experience? We would only keep playing the same sad tunes and reinforcing our emotions about it, too.

We first want to appreciate that it is worthwhile resolving the root causes of our negative thinking. We can do this by letting go of the negative influences and past events where we still feel negatively affected and limited. Working with a Matrix Therapies® Master Practitioner can help us with this. Secondly, a great way to rewrite the stories in our heads is in the form of affirmations.

Affirmations can be future-based for what you want to feel and experience. They can cover how you want to act and what you want to attract instead. Here are some examples of what it can look like to recreate your stories using affirmations:

'I don't like the way my body looks,' can turn into the affirmation of:

'I love and am so grateful for my beautiful body because it gives me so much! It allows me to learn about this physical existence, where I need to look after my body like it is my beloved animal. I learn to treat it with care, and the better I feel about myself, the easier it is to feed it nourishing foods, move it lovingly, and enjoy my continuing relationship with my body. I feel proud to express my body in beautiful clothes, as I love it just the way it is.'

I have this affirmation and more of them in the online journal at www.laurenjobson.com/bookfreecourse

Great and powerful questions can also bring about bigger, better and beautiful thinking, such as:

1. What if I did love and accept myself completely, just as I am now? How would I act today with this love?
2. What would my life look like if I loved and accepted myself completely, just as I am now? Why can't I create and live my life like that today? (You can!)
3. Who would I be if I loved how I looked just as I am now? What emotions would I feel daily if I chose to accept my body as it is today? (It's okay if you want to improve your body appearance at the same time as accepting it. We went over this in Chapter Two with the Acceptance Self Cycle.)
4. How would my life be if I lived according to my heart's priorities?
5. What can I think and believe instead about this situation to make me feel better?

You, of course, can come up with your own powerful questions!

Conclusion of this vow

I vow to talk to myself with perspective, compassion, and forgiveness.

I honour the relationship I have with my judgements and inner voice.

In summary, I highly encourage you to focus on your self-talk by becoming aware of your stories and parenting the parts of you that feel like your stories are true. With your adult perspective, compassion, and forgiveness, you can change your negative default position to be loving, forgiving, and even playful.

As we reflect on self-talk, the stories we tell ourselves and how we can change our words to loving words, we can see that allowing ourselves to think about our past and what might be causing them in the first place, can be changed. Change is possible. It is liberating to know this, and it allows us to step into a new level of life.

Now it's your turn to talk to yourself like your best friend or a loving parent.

A summary of what you learned in
Chapter Five

I Vow to Talk to Myself with Perspective,
Compassion & Forgiveness.
I honour the relationship I have
with my judgements and inner voice.

- ♥ Lauren's story about internal stories of her self-perception
- ♥ Our relationship to our thinking - Our stories are not who we are
- ♥ How is our self-talk created?
- ♥ There is nothing self-loving about believing our stories are true
- ♥ Why do our stories feel so real and true to us?
- ♥ The different kinds of untrue stories – cognitive distortions
- ♥ We default to what is wrong with us
- ♥ Byron Katie's "The Work" – Four Questions
- ♥ How do we speak lovingly to ourselves? - Talk to yourself like a loving parent or best friend
- ♥ Forgiveness is for you
- ♥ How else do we speak lovingly to ourselves? – Create new empowering stories

Devoting yourself to applying the learnings in this chapter:

1. Using the Self-Loving Resources of Tools and Mindset: Grab your journal or the workbook I created for you at www.laurenjobson.com/bookfreecourse

Ask yourself these powerful questions that were asked throughout this chapter and any others you want to add. Go within to listen to what answers come to you and write them down without judgement or questioning. No one else needs to see your answers, so go ahead and deepen your connection to your relationship with your self-talk.

Q1. What kind of negative self-talk do you think you have in your life? Go over the cognitive distortions to see which ones you default to the most.

Q2. What three negative things do you find you say to yourself often?

Q3. What part of your life do you think this negative self-talk stems from?

Q4. Write down three things you could say instead that speak lovingly.

Q5. When you say these new loving words, how do they make you feel?

2. Using the Self-Loving Resource of Support: A Matrix Therapies® and NLP Master Practitioner can help you remove any blocks, such as limiting beliefs and emotions you might have become aware of from this chapter and the questions above.

3. **Using the Self-Loving Resource of Creativity:** Create future focussed, empowering and exciting affirmations for self in replacement to any negative stories. This is similar to a goal setting exercise and what we did from chapter two. I have examples at www.laurenjobson.com/bookfreecourse

4. **Using the Self-Loving Resource of Action:** All of this information in this chapter could just be interesting theory until we devote ourselves to taking applied action. Answer the questions from this chapter and be sure to grab your journal and use the tool of my online course.

5. **Using the Self-Loving Resource of Forgiveness:** This is a reminder that life and self-love is a process. Do what you feel drawn to and practise forgiveness. Particularly self-forgiveness. I also like EFT (emotional freedom technique) for forgiveness as the script is beautiful: "Even though I (state problem), I deeply and completely, love and accept myself". I will share resources on how to do this in my online course at www.laurenjobson.com/bookfreecourse. Again, doing Matrix Therapies® is also wonderful for the practise of forgiveness.

Chapter Six

I Vow to Listen to My Emotions.

I honour the relationship I have with my feelings.

Vow Six

"Our greatest glory is not in never falling, but in rising every time we fall."

CONFUCIUS

Throughout our life, there are many times when we feel utterly rattled, shaken up and our spirit unsettled as we navigate through the problems of being human. When we feel good about things or distract ourselves, we can sometimes forget how raw and painful it is to go through hard times. When we feel pain, we can feel knocked down and alone because the world as we knew it has significantly changed.

One of the biggest struggles in my adult life has been infertility. Now, I am blessed as my journey gave me the biggest blessings. Yet I want to honour it entirely because if I didn't allow myself to share this as the intense struggle it was, I wouldn't be letting the lessons I have learned from it come through. In sharing our journeys of struggle and pain, I have found that we can help others who have felt alone until they heard about our journey. As fellow human beings, we can learn so much from each other.

Before we learn from each other, I think there is a place to learn from ourselves. Our emotions can be our greatest teachers and our wisest guides if we only choose to see them, listen to them, and act appropriately on what they want to tell us.

My experience with infertility has given me an understanding of how sacred it is to let people in when we are hurting. Other people's input, whether in the form of support, advice, listening and sharing, can all contribute to your wellbeing. With the way we listen, hold the emotional space and by what we say and do, we can have a lasting impact on someone.

We were blessed to conceive our daughters with the help of science and medical help. We are incredibly grateful to have two wonderful daughters who are the light of our lives, our new purpose, and our everything. When I wrote this paragraph the first time before my final edit, we were adventuring into our second journey for another child. Today my second daughter is sleeping on my chest in a baby-carrier, as I edit this. Here is what I felt and realised I was doing when we decided to take the IVF path again. I would be playing the most hurtful stories in my mind regarding my inability to conceive again when we were succeeding in all the physical tests with ovulation and sperm count, etc. Still to this day we don't know why we could not fall pregnant naturally, ever.

We had at least twenty-two heartbreaking disappointments in our efforts for our first child. I didn't count for our second child. There were so many intrusive and sometimes painful tests, only to be told the results were fine. Hundreds of blood tests later, I felt my self-identity shifting with what it meant to be a woman, a lover, and a wife who couldn't bring love and a treasured soul into my womb. Somehow, I had become lesser than who I was before because I couldn't do what I most wanted in the world. It was painful to see how others could achieve it so easily and even accidentally. Sometimes, after sex, I would bawl my eyes out, hoping to release the pain which was too overbearing for my body to contain, because the most painful question I had was, 'How is it *our* love and divine connection, through intimacy, couldn't make a baby for us to love?'.

I am being completely real here, I still feel mind blown that such a blessing can come through straightforward sex instead of the hours of travel, traumatic hospital visits, many needles, missed veins, bruises and vaginal probes I went through to have ours. I felt there was something deeply wrong with me and I hated myself for being so jealous of how easy it was for others. Sometimes I still feel this way because that big question above has never been answered for us. The stories we tell ourselves can be endless and utterly soul crushing in the meaning we give to them.

But at the time, it was our truth, and our experience. It is in witnessing the stories we tell ourselves that we can honour the feelings, accept them for what they are and finally, choose to heal them and feel entirely different and resolved.

Sharing this is so personal, raw and achingly vulnerable for me. I don't want to hear another person give me unsolicited advice like "go get drunk, do yoga," or tell me their opinions. They can be so hurtful and even patronising when I didn't ask them for help, let alone when they are not a friend or family member who knows me and deeply cares. I don't want anyone else telling me they wouldn't do IVF because it is "playing God" but then go on to say they "don't judge". I had a nightmare about this concept - our words can be so damaging. Unasked for opinions can ring in your ears even when you disagree. Hence, the words we choose, be as mindful as you can of this. I am mindful in writing this amount in detail, and decided to keep it here, in case you, dear reader, are sadly going through something similar. I want you to know you don't have to feel isolated with whatever experience you are going through. If you have heard some silly things like I did, stay true to what you believe and feel. Create boundaries and discern the rest. People do have good intentions and sometimes you can let them know that all you want is to be heard and seen. Most of the time, most of us need someone to say 'that sucks so much, I am here".

Talk to supportive people who have either gone through what you have or to professionals and people who won't make judgements about your decisions. And if anyone says anything to you along the lines of presuming to know what God thinks - I can tell you God would, of course, want our babies to be born with help from the progression of science and medical intervention. Just like the same people would most likely get medical help to save their life if they fell ill, it is okay to have help with connecting an ovum and sperm together. Conception of a human being is a miracle and a godsend regardless of how the cells join. Who created science after all? I'm grateful to have had some beautiful conversations with my highly devoted Catholic Nan on this topic. We both cried when we thought about the beauty of my daughters and how perfect they are in God's love and divinity. (I don't consider myself Catholic or religious as such, but I do respect religion, God, and have my own relationship to a higher connection).

Your stories and feelings can be completely different to

mine and still be valid; yet somehow, all our pain as fellow humans lead us to realise, we all are in this together. We may have different boats we travel in, but we do weather the same storms. We all feel difficult emotions and struggle at different times in our lives.

The most profound understanding I feel I can share with others through my career in personal development is the concept of the difference between learning and letting go from our experiences, versus, holding on to unresolved stuck and negative emotions for too long. We explore the relationship with our emotions in this chapter.

Our relationship to our emotions - what is the purpose of emotions?

Our emotions are our messengers and greatest guides. They tell us if we are on the path to living in alignment with our values. They also give us messages to learn from and take the appropriate action best for us.

When aligned and fulfilling our core values, we feel happy, passionate, purposeful and content. We can feel a myriad of positive emotions when things are going well for us. When things aren't going so well, it can take a bit more mindfulness and perspective to see how they can help us get back on our path. Or as I like to say, *come back home to ourselves*.

Our negative emotions seem to speak to us the loudest if we are willing to listen to them, by not shutting them out with distractions of technology, addictions of any kind, entertainment, and so on. Instead, choosing to sit with them and pay attention. Sometimes, taking the time to be entertained or distracted can help release some energy. It's not about having to always sit quietly and meditate. We tend to know when we are trying to cover up how we feel over doing what we know we need to.

If we are willing to listen to what they are showing us, we can more easily move through them by understanding what we can learn and what action we need to take to improve and resolve the situation.

My dear friend and pioneer in the field of personal transformation and coaching, the creator of Matrix Therapies® and Archetypal Coaching®, Pip McKay, explains, 'Matrix Therapies is based on the concept that it is important to clear negative emotions to be self-empowered and self-loving. Negative emotions prevent people from gaining success and living to their full potential because they create a focus on the problem and narrow the person's perceptions of solutions. If negative emotions are dealt with effectively, however, they are helpful messages about current situations or past unresolved issues. They are simply meant to be a marker that invites further learnings, changes in behaviour, a need to create boundaries or other actions. Not clearing or healing these emotions can create situations a person wants to avoid. You can use Matrix Therapies® to gain true resolution.'

Below I have outlined the purpose of each negative emotion so we can understand the positive function they can play for us. My intention here, too, is to remind you we all feel these emotions; they are healthy. The most important thing is how we let them dictate our thoughts about ourselves and our lives.

Please note, there are many more derivative emotions from

these mentioned below. Brené Brown, in her book *Atlas of the Heart*, another piece of profound research, shares her exploration of eighty-seven emotions and experiences that define what it means to be human. It is interesting to look into this, as it is fantastic to learn how to communicate with ourselves and others about how we feel and how to label those feelings. We find in our work, we can be more general in our labels for the purpose of resolving all old, stuck and stagnant emotions using Matrix Therapies®.

In our training, we work with what we call the umbrella emotions of anger, sadness, fear, hurt and guilt, since they can hold the same emotional gestalts (forms) inside the unconscious mind. If our unconscious mind were a filing cabinet, it would have many variations of emotions inside the same file. Due to the nature of how the emotions are filed away, a file labelled "fear" could have anxiety, panic, stressed, nervousness, afraid, and petrified inside of it. In this context, a gestalt also means how one emotion is linked together with others, so the same file in the filing cabinet that contains multiple events that made us feel angry would be labelled a gestalt of anger. It is worth being able to label more emotions, as Brené describes, and when we do the healing work we find the umbrella negative emotions to be enough.

Understanding emotions and the lessons they want us to hear

Pip McKay broke down the key umbrella negative emotions into survival emotions, or socialisation emotions.

Survival emotions are the primary emotions of sadness, anger and fear. They aim to trigger particular body responses to help us survive in danger. When our body feels a survival emotion, I like to refer to it as our body wisdom. Our body wisdom responds accordingly to what it feels but not always resourcefully. And this is where the frontal lobe of our brain comes into it. Our awareness of this body response is so important for us to acknowledge so we can distinguish between when we really are in danger or when our body feels like we are, but it is not appropriate to the current situation. We need to act appropriately instead of reacting from a past, unresolved trigger.

A trigger is usually a very intense sensation in the body. It might be a heaviness in our chest, a heat coming from our forehead, a tight feeling or a strong wave in our stomach, a hot flush over our entire body with a racing heart. These are all examples of our body showing up as a sensation, delivering a strong message we can't ignore. These sensations are our emotions speaking to us and most of us need to learn to listen. To do this, we need to label the emotion and have ways to process it resourcefully. These sensations and strong reactions in the body, which are relegated to the mind with the stories we start to tell ourselves, are what we call triggers. Our whole body is literally hooked up in an experience. Generally showing us we have gone back in time to a pain in the past and are yet to resolve.

The hurt and pain in our lives is remembered in the body and sit in our cells, waiting to be released and understood. Just because our conscious mind forgets, our body holds all the meaning we created, particularly as a child between the ages of zero to seven years old. This is the time we are most impressionable and don't have as much freedom as an adult to make choices. Or have the knowledge of the world to know the difference between what is appropriate for us to take on as true, and what is not. Also, choices as to how to act going forward such as what communication is needed, what boundaries are necessary to put in place? How to communicate those boundaries, plus emotional regulation in being able to calm our nervous system down to respond wisely. These are all adult resources we can't always access when we have been triggered. Our body is now functioning from a younger self who is feeling a pain as if we were reliving the experience. The memory won't often come to our mind. But our body remembers.

We want to be aware of our triggers and take full responsibility for them. We can create our lives intentionally instead of just reacting all the time from past programming. I have heard it be said in the personal development world that by the time we are thirty years old, we are a set of patterns – simply programming from our past and that life repeats itself to help us heal.

It is not very often in modern society where our regular sadness, anger and fear are a literal response to danger where our survival is genuinely at stake.

Survival negative emotions

Sadness

Our sadness is generally a message that we have lost something of value to us. Or a disheartening disappointment when an expectation has been unmet. For instance, if a person has a high value of having love and connection (a core human need), fighting with someone they love will cause them to feel sad. Sadness shows us our depth of caring for others, which can be a beautiful way to see it.

Sadness allows us to retreat into our own space to do our healing process while shutting out more interference from the outside world. Since sadness slows down the body and makes us feel like we don't want to do anything, it makes sense that it stops us from putting ourselves in open environments at a time when we don't have the same physiological function that we would usually have without the sadness. It is our body wisdom telling us to take the time to slow down so we can remain safe in our environment.

Grief

Please note that the emotion of grief sits differently than the ones mentioned here in this chapter, as it is more of a process than any other emotion. Grief could be categorised under sadness. Yet, it also encompasses many other survival emotions, such as anger, fear, maybe guilt, etc., amongst the feeling of loss and is very personal to each person.

In our coaching and training, we use and teach a Grief Script in Matrix Therapies®, which Pip McKay created. We use it to help the person become more functional if they feel the grief is hindering their everyday living and want to find some ease with it. Unlike the other emotions in Matrix Therapies®, where we can reframe them at any stage and intend to resolve them completely. With grief, we are looking to help the person ease some of the energy in it, according to where they are at in the journey. I had one of my biggest client breakthroughs when I helped a woman acknowledge and resolve her grief, which was eight years after her mother had passed away. It was the right time for her to release this amount of emotion from her body.

What we do want to understand with grief is it is common to feel that having grief equals love for the person who we have lost. Like if we stop grieving for them, we somehow think it would mean we don't love them enough or have stopped loving them. This is not true. Love equals love. Pip McKay states this reframe, and we can use this if someone is ready to hear it in the coaching context. Another reframe is the person who is no longer with us wouldn't want us to grieve and be in pain for too long. Instead, they would want us to be happy and enjoy our lives. Again, these points need to be considered with care, compassion, and mindfulness so the grieving person can feel what they feel and process it in their own way and time.

Keep in mind our unconscious mind wants us to let go of feelings that cause restriction of energy and blood flow in the body. So, there does come a time when it is best for the person to process the emotion until it is no longer a painful, stagnant, and stuck feeling in their body. Being able to talk about the person who was lost with smiles and laughter for the memories shared is one example of this being healthier on the body.

Anger

Our anger, just like sadness, is a survival emotion. It triggers our body wisdom to respond with efforts to keep us safe in the face of perceived or actual danger. As sadness creates stillness, anger creates action. This is a generalisation here, so this is only sometimes true; many women can repress anger underneath their sadness. It can be easier for them to express sadness than it is to feel anger. Sometimes this stems from what they think they are permitted to feel by society. And men are often the opposite. Where they can repress sadness underneath their anger. They can more easily express anger because they think they are less likely to be permitted by society to feel sad. Hopefully, this is changing as we learn to express our emotions in the most resourceful ways possible.

Anger helps us learn our personal boundaries and shows us what is important to us (our values, of course). Since this emotion arises when our boundaries are crossed, it shows us our triggers when we need to defend ourselves and when change needs to happen for us to feel better about situations.

Since our values drive our judgements of ourselves and others, it is crucial to notice the actual trigger for our anger. To understand the value that needs to be fulfilled and take the appropriate action.

Fear

Fear, of course, helps us fly away or fight danger. It can also give us a paralysing response by freezing us, which could be helpful in a situation where you saw a snake. Yet totally crushing if you get stage fright (been there before with a speech I didn't prepare for. I don't recommend not preparing!).

When it comes to fear, there is also the fear of stepping out into the unknown. In other words, "stepping out of our comfort zone.". You may have heard how crucial it is to step out of what you have known, your familiar comfort zone, to experience the next level of potential. The chances are high that to improve our lives in any area means we will need to embrace a certain level of uncertainty and fear to do something new and different. How much we feel our fear and do it anyway, step into our courage and confidence will determine our next level of success in achieving what we want.

Anxiety

Anxiety is using our imagination to picture and make movies of future events not going well. It is an anticipation of something going wrong. This can come from imagining what has happened in our past could happen again. Or it could be we have yet to experience an event occurring before, and with the uncertainty, we picture it going unsuccessfully.

Anxiety can be so unconscious we aren't aware of the movies we are playing in our minds. Since the feeling has become so second nature to some, the nervous system operates in constant fear mode, so we have automatic fearful body responses whilst the mind feels totally out of control. The mind wants to solve a perceived future problem to keep us safe.

It is in using our imagination to envision things working out well and successfully where anxiety can diminish. It is having faith in our future self and trusting that things will be okay. It is easier to have faith and to trust in the future when we have resolved our pains from our past, so our nervous system is not in overdrive or as sensitive anymore. We resolve this pain from our past by parenting ourselves out of the emotion we still feel in the present. Just like we do with all the built-up emotions mentioned in this chapter. I like working with my own coach in Matrix Therapies® to do this for myself. I help my clients resolve their emotional gestalts too. It's a pleasant and quick process, most are surprised to learn and experience.

Socialisation negative emotions

There are three basic socialisation negative emotions: hurt, embarrassment and guilt. They are categorised as socialisation emotions because we can only have them by interacting with others.

Hurt
The positive purpose of hurt is to stop us from repeating harmful and unhealthy interactions with others. If we are hurt in a specific circumstance or event, the purpose of emotion (not just hurt but any emotion) is to generalise the experience and link it to a particular meaning.

For example, when a person is hurt by being rejected in a relationship, they may generalise relationships to have a meaning of being painful. This may cause the person to avoid getting into intimate relationships or taking initial steps like dating. The pain of unresolved hurt still lies in their unconscious mind. Making them feel they can't trust love, for instance. If this person chose to resolve their past hurts, they would consequently find it easier to have positive beliefs about this area of life. Allowing them to have a different, more positive experience.

The hurt I was holding on to stopped me from contacting my older sisters for a long time. What a loss that was!

Embarrassment
Embarrassment helps control our behaviours whilst we are

with other people. Whilst embarrassment has the positive intent of stopping us from doing inappropriate behaviours that could offend others. If we have too much of it, it can prevent us from feeling like we can relax and be ourselves.

Shame
Shame shows us we may be internalising what we think others believe of us and not feeling lovable or good enough to be accepted by them. Brené Brown states that guilt is feeling bad about a behaviour, whereas shame is the deep feeling of thinking there must be something inherently wrong with us.

Brené's 2010 TED talk, which brought her to the public eye as a researcher, spoke about "The Power of Vulnerability", where she shares about being vulnerable enough to share with those close to you the stories you are playing in your head.

Guilt
Guilt prevents us from hurting others or repeatedly behaving in a way that hurts others. The interesting thing with guilt is sometimes people are afraid to own their behaviours and the pain they have inflicted on others. What they can do is start to blame the person they hurt and continue to act inappropriately towards them. This is an example of a behaviour wanting to protect a hurt part of themselves when what really needs to happen is to have enough courage and humility to heal themselves. Being able to not project unresolved pain onto others, instead, taking responsibility for actions and to apologise.

Guilt is a message to learn from our behaviour, make amends if necessary, and to do better next time. When we commit to learning from our mistakes and behaving differently, there is no reason to hold on to guilt. Holding on to guilt doesn't make us a better person. Letting it go and acting appropriately in the future does.

Now what we need to understand about our negative emotions is the difference between a healthy presence of them and what we can learn from them, compared to a build-up of unresolved negative feelings we have not resolved from the past.

Our pasts are meant to be resourceful, not emotional

When we think of a memory from the past, and we can notice our learnings instead of feeling emotional in the present, this is having our pasts be resourceful, not emotional. If we are still triggered, which is feeling the emotion in our body in the present moment, this is unresolved. Instead, we want to be able to remember the *learnings* from past events whilst not being emotional about them. In other words, our body should not react with a negative sensation or behavioural response.

Being unresolved is when we don't connect to our feminine energy and listen to what we could learn from our experiences. It is when we still feel stuck back in times of sadness, anger, fear, hurt, guilt and so on, and our past selves affect us in the now. Consequently, taking them into our futures too.

Emotions are a process

Emotions show up in the body first as a sensation. A lot of the time, the feeling in the body is a trigger from a memory that happened to us much earlier in our lives. Our inner children are stored in our bodies, and we project their unresolved stories onto our current situation. We then have a place of choice. Do we explore the actual cause of our body's memory trigger? Or do we blame the external circumstance for what is going on? If we take the time to reflect on what our emotions want to tell us and what it reminds us of, we will likely find it is an inner child or past self who needs us as our adult selves to parent them.

There are times when the emotion is appropriate for the current event. Reflection, listening to the feeling and then appropriately taking the most mature and resourceful action is required. Connecting with our power if something is not right and self-loving for us to accept, we must put our boundaries in place and do something about it. If the emotion is coming from a past self, since we had less adult resources to deal with the event back then, we become unresourceful in the present. We wouldn't find it easy to put up a boundary for example, because our body is functioning from a younger self.

This happened to me when Brendon and I moved into the home we bought and renovated, just before our wedding when we had already been together for eight years. I was in the laundry one day, taking out the clothes from the washing machine and putting them into the dryer. He called out, 'Did you check the lint filter?' My blunt response was, 'Of course, I f**n checked the lint filter; what do you think of me? Do you think I'm an idiot?' This was, of course, a completely unwarranted, and uncalled for response. Firstly, Brendon and I would never accept swearing at each other as that is basic respect out the window. Also, why was I yelling at him like this because of a simple question? He said he was just saying it as a little reminder and had no thought of relating it to my intellect. Yet I had responded from a build-up of unresolved emotion in me involving how I chose not to feel good enough. The context of soon becoming his wife and moving in together presented a trigger from a belief I had created about what he might expect of me. My inner child projected this belief onto him and all of my "not good enough" feelings of anger around this came out. I definitely needed to resolve this within myself, so I would not blame my partner for my own unresolved pain.

The above example is an obvious one where it could be apparent to most people that the problem I had was never about how I did the laundry. Hopefully, only a few of these events happen in any relationship before someone takes responsibility for their triggers, resolves them and changes the unresourceful behaviour. But there are plenty of other responses people have where they project something onto others which are entirely out of their awareness when it is about something deeper and from their past that is influencing their reactions and behaviours.

Then there are times when we might first think we are rattled by the circumstance we are in. Yet what is actually happening is we are being triggered by something unresolved from the past. We can usually tell if our response is bigger than the event itself when not facing what needs to be done to rectify the situation.

For example, I was friends with a married couple many years ago. I had a closer relationship to the man because I had formed a friendship with him before I had with his wife. He felt like a brother to me because our energies were similar, and we really understood each other. One day, I was speaking to her on the phone and she brought up with me how he was a little "perturbed" I hadn't given him certain credit in a work thing I had created. I was immediately triggered and naturally, at the time, didn't realise why I was feeling such a strong sensation in my body. I was aware straight away of the self-talk of "why isn't he just telling me himself if it's not a big deal to him, yet it is being mentioned by her?!" I acted fine but soon after the phone call, I didn't handle this situation well in my communication going forward as my full body response was to be repelled from further relationship with either of them. My behaviour was to cut off communication completely.

The fact I wasn't willing to deal with it by open communication to resolve my feelings, showed me with time, that this was something bigger for me. I needed to have been vulnerable enough to face my pain and talk to them if I was to heal this inside of me.

Some time had passed and I realised in my evaluation, this dynamic felt like a complete repeat of losing my relationship with my half-brother, who I met when I was sixteen. I didn't want to repeat the hurt again of losing a brother because of "a woman's interference". Also him not standing up for me or fighting to hold on to a relationship with me – even though my friend did in a way – I just wanted to avoid the situation entirely. I wanted to be the one in control of any pain I would feel, so I chose to part ways because it was the best I could do at the time. I only regret hurting their feelings. I knew I could have handled it better if I wasn't so deeply triggered from my past.

This is a clear example of first thinking my emotions were coming from the event itself since I don't find it comfortable at all to be accused of something I didn't do and wished it came directly from him. Yet, it felt much deeper than this and my extreme behaviour of cutting off the relationships was all to do with a past situation with my older brother I no longer have a relationship with. I went back to my own personal Matrix Therapies® Coach to work on this by clearing the influence of my brother and now I am completely at peace with it all.

When our partner, child, friend, family member – whoever or whatever in the external world "makes us" angry, sad, or any other negative emotion, it is a good idea to ask ourselves the following questions:

1. What is it about their behaviour that makes me feel___?
2. How does what they are doing cause me to feel___?
3. What do I need to understand about myself in this emotion that will allow me to know what needs to be healed in me?
4. What do I need to understand about myself in this emotion to allow me to know what specifically needs to be communicated to the other person involved?
5. Do I need to parent myself here in this situation, and will that change how I react to what is going on, without the other person needing to change?
6. Do I need to communicate how the other person involved can adapt their behaviour too, and come to an understanding or agreement on how we can best meet each other's needs?

Emotional logic versus intellectual logic

Emotional logic is entirely different to our intellectual logic and reasoning. This means our emotions sometimes seem irrational, disproportionate, and seemingly make no sense to our thinking minds. Emotional logic works in two ways:

1) Cause and Effect:
It functions like this: If "Cause" happens, then "Effect" will happen. Suppose a past emotional event has not been resolved. In that case, the emotions will continue to function from anything that seems like the external trigger (the cause), believing it will have the same effect (outcome).

For example, a person has felt rejected in the past. The emotional logic functions from a place of fearing rejection again. Regardless of the intellectual logic of it being a new and different relationship, the person finds themselves creating many ways to prevent themselves from being rejected again, creating walls in their new relationship, avoiding vulnerability and hence, stopping true intimacy. It doesn't make any logical sense since the behaviour which wants to protect them is actually creating ways to not have a relationship at all. Resolving this past pain and any linked limiting beliefs is worth resolving so this fear no longer drives perceptions, brings up negative emotions or creates sabotaging behaviours.

2) Complex Equivalence:
This is when we link one thing to mean another. Slightly different to "Cause and Effect," this one is about connecting two things and perceiving them to be intrinsically linked

simultaneously - causing false identifications and meanings to external stimuli.

The moment we make an identification, we are linking ourselves to a particular meaning which could very likely be untrue.

For example, once an external circumstance creates negative emotions that are then built up over time, they generalise and become a limiting belief to sit in the function of such equations like:

- relationships = rejection
- relationships = pain
- "I" inside of a relationship = not good enough
- "I" = am not lovable

Even if we can intellectually rationalise external circumstances as not meaning anything, they can drive us unconsciously if we don't resolve our past emotions. To change our emotional logic, we need to be self-aware enough to know if we are functioning, behaving, thinking, feeling from unresolved pain in the past, or if we are already able to deal with each new circumstance through the eyes of the resourceful and lovable adults we are today.

If our emotions take over our present experience, it is our inner children/past selves speaking up to be understood. Our emotions want us to have our present self, parent and listen to them. It is like we are rescuing our past selves from being stuck in our bodies in that past circumstance. Matrix Therapies® allows us to connect to these unresolved parts of us and to resource them with insight into who we want to be today.

A Matrix Therapies® Master Practitioner can help with this. I think we all need to cleanse our "emotional baggage" regularly. In more loving and real terms, getting rid of our emotional baggage is loving and accepting every part of us who has gone through what we have, seeing our past selves, honouring their experience and guiding them into who we are today. There isn't anything more self-loving than that.

Seeing our emotions

I have created an acronym for seeing our emotions and processing them. I have played on the spelling and made it to S.E.A. our emotions.

S.E.A. stands for:
 S. You can be still but it's not always completely necessary. What *is* necessary is to simply notice the **sensation** in your body. Also, notice the **stories and self-talk** you have about this **sensation**. Is your heart beating faster than normal? How does your stomach feel? Do you have any heat or tightness in your body? These are all your body's way of sharing a message with you.

What is our self-talk saying about why we feel this emotion? Next...

E. Emote the **energy** with **evaluation.** It is okay, safe and you have permission to feel what you do in your body at any time. Once you allow it to be in your body as it is, connect with your body to emote and embody this feeling. It will be time to gently evaluate it.

Evaluate, means to notice what emotion it is by choosing a label for how you feel. Is it anxiety? Is it anger? Is it sadness or something different?

Notice if this is a trigger from a past experience? Or from a lack of something in the present such as boundaries or effective communication? Or could it be a worry about something yet to happen in the future?

Emote by resourcefully feeling it through your body and processing it. I've heard of emotions being referred to as energy in motion. You can find resourceful, beautiful ways to emote it (to express it). You can do this by writing things down, going for a walk, dancing, doing a Matrix Therapies® process with a therapist, or sitting still with your thoughts and feelings.

Label the emotion. Evaluate what it is about and identify where the story and self-talk is coming from.

Then...

A. Acknowledge the feeling. **Accept** and **allow** it for what it is. Then **act accordingly.**

We can accept emotions as they are so we stop finding ways to escape their uncomfortableness. If you have done the first two steps in seeing them, emoting and evaluating them, it is essential to note in the evaluation part of this process, go gently. Not being judgemental but seeing and treating yourself like you would lovingly respond to a cherished child. It is important to give permission to yourself to have emotions. This is allowing the emotion to be there. Be a loving and accepting parent to your inner children, just like you would want to be a loving parent to your biological children. We were all children, after all, and because time has us grow older physically, we need to help our emotional selves grow up, too, through nurturing and loving care.

Finally, taking action is needed to resolve them and move on. Resourceful action is what I am referring to here, as it can only be best for you if the previous steps have been completely honoured. We need to heal our triggers by taking full responsibility for our feelings and reactions. Giving permission and letting them know it is safe to feel all these feelings. When we can do this, we can take the learning to remember and integrate it into what we do next. We then have new perspectives and can adjust our behaviours accordingly.

Sense in my body what is going on. Eg. Fast heartbeat, tight chest, whirling stomach, heat on forehead and so on. Notice the **stories and self-talk** I have in my mind about this **sensation**.

Emote the energy by allowing it to be in my body. **Evaluate** where it comes from and label the emotions. Is it a trigger from a past experience? From a lack of resources in the present? Or a future worry?

Acknowledge. Accept and **allow** the emotions as they are. It is safe and okay to feel this. Give permission for it to be there as it is.
Act accordingly and appropriately.

my emotions

I have then taken the acronym a step further. Let's ask ourselves, what emotions do we want to take seat in our hearts and bodies going forward? We can only really know if we have moved on from an emotional event when we look back at the event, and in our bodies, we can't bring up a negative response or feeling. We have transformed the emotion into either a neutral feeling or entirely into a different emotion, such as anger into understanding, sadness into compassion, and fear into courage. What emotions do we want to hold in our hearts long term? Which ones will we allow to take a seat there in our bodies?

Imagine then the resources we could tap into when we can look back on things with a new perspective and with a transformed emotion, too? We have S.E.A. for the first three steps and we take it one step further with T for Transform.

What emotions do we want to take S.E.A.T. in our hearts and bodies?

S. You can be still but it's not always completely necessary. What *is* necessary is to simply notice the **sensation** in your body. Also, notice the **stories and self-talk** you have about this **sensation**.

E. Emote the **energy** with **evaluation**.

A. Acknowledge the feeling. **Accept** and **allow** it for what it is and **act accordingly**.

T. Transform the feelings into neutrality or an entirely different emotion. Once we take action by communicating, boundaries, or letting it go inside of us. You may need further support for those bigger, significant, emotional events by working with a Matrix Therapies® Master Practitioner or experiencing and learning Matrix Therapies® at our training. Matrix Therapies® allows us to transform an emotion like anger into understanding, sadness into compassion, or fear into courage. It can also help us let go of any energetic charge from the body.

 **Sense** in my body what is going on. Eg. Fast heartbeat, tight chest, whirling stomach, heat on forehead and so on. Notice the **stories and self-talk** I have in my mind about this **sensation.**

 Emote the energy by allowing it to be in my body. **Evaluate** where it comes from and label the emotions. Is it a trigger from a past experience? From a lack of resources in the present? Or a future worry?

 Acknowledge. Accept and **allow** the emotions as they are. It is safe and okay to feel this. Give permission for it to be there as it is.
Act accordingly and appropriately.

 **Transform** it into a neutral sensation and emotion in the body.
Work with a Matrix Therapies® Coach to help clear it from the body entirely.

Conclusion of this vow

I vow to listen to my emotions.
I honour the relationship I have with my feelings.

Emotions take whatever time to process you want them to take. It's personal and unique to each person and circumstance. The only thing about some people taking longer to process emotions is whether they are processing it by wanting to heal and nurture themselves through it versus those who aren't willing to consider letting go or are stuck for unconscious reasons. One of these reasons is wanting to remain a victim so as to gain significance - a core human need. Sometimes people like to hold on to emotion because they feel significant (unique or special) in having their problem and feel there are greater benefits in having the problem than they perceive in the benefits of solving it. When I look back on my stomach ache problem as a teenager, I can see I was getting a lot of attention and having good excuses for getting out of things I didn't want to do. I didn't know this or do this consciously. It is called having a secondary gain. Often, people are so secure and certain (both core human needs) of their problems that the uncertainty or perceived difficulty involved in the solution, makes them feel resistant to change. Also, our ego, which is a part of us who wants to protect us, could be wanting to feel right. We can be so attached to feeling right we are willing to hold on to negativity so as not to be challenged in being wrong.

What is important about understanding all the information from this chapter is the most positive, happy, and successful people still feel all of these negative emotions at times. The difference between them and others who don't fulfil their potential is they don't allow negative emotions to stop them from loving themselves. They listen to their emotions, even the negative ones, learn from them and let them go. This allows them to take the right actions needed to improve their lives.

A summary of what you learned in
Chapter Six

I vow to listen to my emotions.
I honour the relationship I have with my feelings.

- Lauren's story of infertility
- Our relationship to our emotions - what is the purpose of emotions?
- Understanding emotions and the lessons they want us to hear
- Survival negative emotions
- Socialisation negative emotions
- Our pasts are meant to be resourceful, not emotional
- Emotions are a process
- Emotional logic versus intellectual logic
- Seeing our emotions with S.E.A.
- What emotions do we want to take S.E.A.T. in our hearts and bodies?

Devoting yourself to applying the learnings in this chapter:

1. **Using the Self-Loving Resource of a Tool:** Print out the diagrams I have for you at www.laurenjobson.com/bookfreecourse of S.E.A.ing our emotions and them taking S.E.A.T in our bodies. Put them in a place where you can look at them daily to remind you of the process whilst you are still learning to slow down and pay attention to your emotions more often.

2. **Using the Self-Loving Resource of Support:** A Matrix Therapies® and NLP Master Practitioner can help you remove any blocks, such as limiting beliefs and emotions you might have become aware of from this chapter. The first thing a Master Practitioner will encourage, is to do negative influence clearing of others and then to resolve the emotional gestalts of the umbrella emotions and any other emotions you may still be holding on to from the past.

3. **Using the Self-Loving Resource of Forgiveness:** This is a reminder that life and self-love is a process. Do what you feel drawn to and practise forgiveness. Particularly self-forgiveness. I also like EFT (emotional freedom technique) for forgiveness as the script is beautiful: "Even though I (state problem), I deeply and completely, love and accept myself". I will share resources on how to do this in my online course. Again, doing Matrix Therapies® is also wonderful for the practise of forgiveness.

Chapter Seven

I Vow to Honour My Own Path and to Trust in the Big Picture of My Life.

I honour the relationship I have with a higher connection to myself.

Vow Seven

*"We don't have a sole purpose.
We have a soul purpose."*

LAUREN JOBSON

I remember the weekend I met myself. I deeply reconnected and understood the parts of me that make me who I am. It was a moment of pure joy and gratitude. I felt like I had come home to myself. I was on a break in a weekend training called "Evolve Now! Level 1A: Passion and Purpose Coaching" created and taught by Pip McKay.

I stood outside to breathe in the fresh air on a warm summer's day. It was a comfortable day, not as humid as Sydney can get. A pleasant breeze cooled my skin. I looked up at the blue sky and felt the world brighten around me. I had found myself. I had a feeling life was going to get so much better. And sure enough, it did.

I realised, looking back, the things in my life that weren't successful for me had been an uphill battle. I hadn't acknowledged just how much of a struggle I was making things. I didn't know how my career, for example, could be much more enjoyable and successful than I had allowed myself.

I accepted my path as a struggle. I thought it was just the way it would be.

I was keeping myself in a bubble of delusion, thinking all I needed to do was to keep taking action. Yet my actions didn't seem to align with who I was. Things felt hard, and no matter how much effort I was putting into my journey, I wasn't getting much to show for it.

The most significant example was in my coaching and training business. From a young age, I was lucky enough to feel a deep yearning for what made me feel alive and full of purpose. I wanted to learn about human potential and then share this beauty with others through teaching NLP and coaching. I took all the steps to pursue my passion. Yet, I was unable to make it my full-time business simply because of my actions. I was not making much money, so you could say it was more of a passion project. Nowadays called a side hustle. I didn't realise this; hence, I was disillusioned. It meant that I was working other jobs, such as babysitting, that had nothing to do with the same industry I wanted to be in. I would be making money from these different jobs to pay for my client room hire, coaching website and business cards, because such things made me feel I was running a business.

Don't get me wrong, building up your business whilst working other jobs to bring in the money in the early stages is a great strategy; I recommend it. It is excellent not to put financial pressure on the business when you are just finding your way. But for me, this wasn't the problem. It was like I had already decided I could not make great money doing what I love. I was unconsciously stopping myself from investing myself and all my energy into it.

Bless my darling website designer, who happens to be a close friend from high school too. Over the years, I asked her to change my website repeatedly before I felt I could share it. It was never the website that was the problem. I changed my tagline; I needed a better logo, to get better photos. It just went on and on with why it wasn't ready to be seen. My business name was "Results with Lauren" - looking back now, I know I felt embarrassed about the name. It didn't feel like me, but I couldn't pinpoint this at the time. I did not feel excited about sharing it with others. Woah – a big problem right there when I felt embarrassed to share the name of my business!

I remember one parent of a child I was looking after at my babysitting job, on receiving my business card, asked me, 'Oh, so are you a maths tutor?' Oh, dear! "Results with Lauren" came across as a maths tutor. I kept the name. Again, this was a big sign from the universe, yet I remained disillusioned. I couldn't see past what was holding me back.

Fast forward to the weekend where I met myself. All of this was about to change in a liberating and inspiring way. The entire process was enjoyable and empowering, and only years later, did I truly realise how disillusioned I had been. Such is the nature of unconscious limitations holding us back.

That weekend, at the "Evolve Now! Level 1A: Passion and Purpose Coaching" training, I learned the three authentic energies that make up who I am. I discovered when I am living in these archetypal energies, I am most passionate, most authentically me and through them, I contribute who I am meant to be. I learned my soul chose these three archetypes to live through, creating a guided path of self-fulfilment and contribution.

We learned that our purpose is not to do one thing, and only when we find that one thing, to fill up our time with that. But rather, our purpose is to be the most authentic version of ourselves and bring our true self to whatever it is we do. We contribute to others and help the world by pursuing the things we are passionate about with all our unique traits, skills and gifts.

I then discovered my talent archetype, the energy I have become most skilled in and what I specifically get paid to do. Once we discover the three Passion and Purpose Archetypes, we identify the Talent Archetype. Then we discover the order they have inside of us which makes up our genius flow. Our genius flow means when we follow a particular order of these energies, we bring passion to everything we do. Pip McKay created this structure, and these profound coaching processes were informed by her twenty-two-year spiritual apprenticeship in ancient wisdom.

I found out my four Archetypes are:

- The Lovers,
- The Creative Nurturer,
- The Innocent Adventurer and
- The Knight.

After this weekend, I immediately changed my business name to "Love Life with Lauren", because one of my archetypes, The Lovers Archetype, is all about love, intimate connection, and self-love. I could also quickly develop my tagline and business message when I worked with the energies of my other archetypes. "Inspiring and Nurturing a Happier You" is informed by my Innocent Adventurer, which is all about inspiration. The Creative Nurturer is all about nurturing. Now, beyond a business name and some branding help, this was about truly feeling aligned with who I am and loving what I do. My business is now an authentic expression of me.

I then went on to do the Evolve Now! Level 1B: Masculine & Feminine Coaching training where I changed my parental programming. This included resolving one belief I had from my perception of what I observed from my parents that: "the man in the relationship should earn most of the money." As a result, my side hustle finally became a full-time business. It has been what I do to support myself financially ever since. I have also been able to make more money than my husband which doesn't mean anything except the proof I made a significant change. I now have my own Training School where I offer different training options, including these weekend training courses:

Evolve Now! Level 1A: Passion and Purpose Coaching
Evolve Now! Level 1B: Masculine and Feminine Coaching
Evolve Now! Level 1C: Matrix Therapies® Coaching

My Personal Development Training Company is called "Intuitive Heart Training Academy" (yes, there is a particular aligned reason for this name, too), and my one-to-one coaching business still exists as "Love Life with Lauren."

Let's go into more information about the Archetypal work I offer so you can see how you could also meet yourself at the deepest level. I find the archetypal work we do is all about connecting to the best parts of us and a way to connect with our soul. To me, it is one aspect of my spiritual understanding and practice. Spirituality means to me, a way we stay in awe and in connection with our most true and powerful selves whilst also being connected to something greater than ourselves.

This chapter is about our soul's purpose, connection to

universal consciousness and spirituality. Spirituality can mean any beliefs you have that take you beyond this physical realm of our five senses, with a focus beyond self. For some, it could be a religion, for others, it could be their belief that there is a bigger purpose and meaning to our physical existence on earth. It is entirely personal to each of us.

Our relationship to living our daily lives by contributing to the bigger picture of who we came here to be

We are human beings with a body, emotions, intellect, and spirit. Up until this point, we have examined how we process our world and make meaning of our outside world with how it affects us internally. It is now time to look at how our behaviours and even the energy we express in the world are crucial to changing our lives and creating a life that is most self-loving.

It is a high value of mine and part of my purpose to encourage us to question whether our contribution to this world is either adding to the light of human consciousness or adding to the shadow. Are we creating more light in our lives, or are we creating more pain, struggle, and darkness?

With our work with "Evolve Now! Level 1A: Passion and Purpose Coaching", we see that when you live inside the energies of your soul's three archetypes, you always bring more light to the world simply by being your most passionate, happy and authentic self. How do we know our most passionate, happy and authentic selves? Our Archetypal identity uncovers this for us.

Our authentic archetypal energies

An Archetype is a universal, symbolic idea, that is innate. In Pip McKay's work, since she experientially studied Archetypes for over twenty years, and used them successfully for nearly 40 years today, teaches the Archetypes in their ideal form from the ancient wisdom with how they were shared and intended (not to be confused with stereotypes). So, an Archetype is a symbolic idea of something, that is universally understood from birth and is in its ideal form. Carl Jung described it well when he said it's like if we asked one hundred people to define something with one hundred different meanings, there would be common words and those would be the archetypal nature of the thing.

For example, a tree. Some meaning people would have said are from their own personal memories about a tree, remembering when they were young and swinging from a tree. Other meaning would be cultural such as the cherry blossom tree in Japan signifies the fleeting nature of life. The common answers between the one hundred different people like, life, nature, mother earth, life giving, life cycles, growth – these are the archetypal meanings of a tree. The Archetype of Mother would be things like, unconditional love, nurture, safety, security, warmth, gentle and so on. When we know the Archetype, we have a way to understand how we create negative emotions in relation to how much of our innate knowing and expectation of what a mother should be like versus our actual experience of mother. The more we experience close to the ideal of mother, the more fulfilled and happier we feel. The further away our own mum was to the ideal of mother, the more negative emotions, and beliefs we would have. Every one of us is born having innate expectations of how we should do certain things as humans and 'play' different roles. When you hear the words "Innocent Adventurer" there is a deep sense that we all have the ability to be childlike, innocent, free, go on adventures, be inspired and so on. This is another Archetype.

At the Archetypal Coaching Weekend Training, "Evolve Now Level 1A: Passion and Purpose Coaching", we use a process that takes us out of our adult intellectual mind, with its built-up influences of others' emotions, and limitations; things that are not true to who we are; and seeks to connect with the deepest parts of who we are with as little external and outside influence as possible. This process is crucial to discover our soul's archetypes effectively.

We have you discover the three archetypes your soul chose for you to express. Then there is a fourth archetype, your Talent Archetype, which is the energy and skills you have learned to be good at in this lifetime and is specifically what you get paid to do.

I can share with you my Genius Flow with my four archetypes below so you can have an idea of how helpful this is:

1. Firstly, I need to feel a **connection** as I come to **deeply see** the other person, myself or a specific idea in a **beautiful** vision (**The Lovers** Archetype)
2. Secondly, this connection leads me to become **inspired** by an **idea**, and I **gain the energy** to **embark** on a **new adventure** (**The Innocent Adventurer** Archetype)
3. I can then **nurture** that connection and idea into a **creation** by using my **imagination** wisely, which will

be of **service to help others** (**The Creative Nurturer** Archetype)
4. To finally **achieve** a mutual **goal** in that connection and **get a result** (**The Knight** Archetype – my Talent Archetype)

Above is my Genius Flow, a concept created by Pip McKay. It allows us to come back into flow and helps us resolve challenges, problems or obstacles by living through the light of the archetypal energy. Our archetypal work teaches how archetypes give us an ideal template of living in this energy or essence in its most ideal form, which comes with many incredibly helpful resources. We also learn the shadow aspects of each archetype to shed light on any problems. This also helps us know which archetype has the most appropriate resources to solve each problem. Every archetype has a secret to our success, love and happiness and a key to help us unlock the resources of that archetype.

Let me explain through an example. The Lovers Archetype secret to success, love and happiness is "Discernment", and self-love is the key to unlocking the resource of discernment. Simply put, The Lovers Archetype teaches us that when we love ourselves enough and come from the most self-loving position to discern what is best for us, it will also be best for everyone else involved. It allows us to decide what to keep in our lives and what to cut away and let go of, which we looked at in Chapter Four when we went through our relationship with our power.

I go through each of the eight possible Passion and Purpose Archetypes, their secrets, and keys at my online free live event. You can register your place for the next one at www.laurenjobson.com/free-event

There are many paths to our passions and purpose

Whatever our interests, I think we are all called to answer the following universal questions at least once in our lives: What is my life's purpose? Why was I born? What is my life for? What is my unique contribution to this world? What is the purpose of pain and struggle? These are huge questions, and I think the way we come to answer them is personal to each of us.

The Archetypes I share here are just one way (yet a very profound and powerful way) to guide us back home to ourselves and uncover our path to purpose. Some other ways that guide us to our most authentic self and purpose are to learn more about our birth charts through Astrology, Human Design and Gene Keys. They also come from ancient wisdom like Archetypes and are intertwined with layers of profound knowledge to explore the resources and principles that make up human consciousness. I am deepening my understanding of these and find them highly fascinating and insightful in accurately answering why we are the way we are and how to solve problems. The principles of consciousness also have the answers to any problem, from money worries to relationship conflicts, feeling lost with no direction or any pain we experience in human existence. The principles can't solve our problems without our participation and action, but they can show us how to do so.

I am guiding people through this information in my 1 to 1 coaching. I encourage those who feel called to be aligned with all the principles that make up human consciousness to experience our three-weekend retreats training called Evolve Now! Level 2. I share information on this during my free online events. You can find the next one at www.laurenjobson.com/free-event

These models and mediums which shine a light on our most authentic nature, all show that our soul comes with a blueprint of energy, a pathway if you like, that we can work alongside to fulfil our highest potential. We want to honour our path as it works with our free will and gives us our ideal alignment to joy, purpose and fulfilment.

What does it mean to honour our own path?

Firstly, since the word "honour" means to have high respect and regard for something (which I discussed in the introduction of this book). In order to honour our own path we need to take a deeper look into what our "own path" means.

Our "own path" is our unique life's journey. It is our individual experience of what we came here to live. A path implies that we can either be on it or go off track. I find this to be a powerful metaphor since it presupposes a few things for us.

We can presume the following:

1) If we have our own path, we can assume our path is important for us to take. It can imply we have a purpose to fulfil.

For most of my life, I've had a belief that we all have a calling, a purpose and a destiny. When I was little, I remember feeling connected to something outside me as I felt watched over and guided. It would come in flashing moments where I would envision myself as an adult and feel how this moment in my childhood would somehow become significant. Indeed, many memories stand out vividly in my mind from when I was younger. I can remember how I felt and what I was thinking. With some reflection, they have informed many of my positive beliefs about who I am today.

As I grew older, I loved coming across books and teachings about the idea that we are souls who chose to live in this human body and experience certain things for a reason. This idea that we chose our body, our family, even our problems for the purpose of experiencing what our soul wanted to learn by having a human existence. I now teach this concept and the path that lead me to do so has confirmed my feelings that something divine is occurring for me and not to me. Of course, this wasn't always a concept that gave me peace or was easy when I was going through something painful. Only afterwards, in resolving the problem, could I see this knowing of divine support helped me have a greater perspective of my problems and struggles.

Having a faith, whether religion or another set of beliefs, gives a higher perspective on our lives and supports how we are guided on our path.

I ask you;

- ♥ What do you think your "own path" means?
- ♥ What do you believe about having your own path to follow?

- What do you believe about destiny?
- What does having a purpose mean to you?

2) If we have our own path, we can assume we create it.
Considering your beliefs about what your "own path" means to you, I wonder if you have felt there was a path you were just born into, a path already laid out in front of you? Suppose you believe in having a connection to a higher divinity, a higher power. Could you notice even if you feel what you've experienced has just happened to you, can you see that a lot of the path you have walked, as an adult, has been made up of many of your own choices? We don't choose everything that happens to us. I do believe we choose how we respond and who we become from it.

It is like you are on a beautiful bush walk, somewhere you have heard about as being a regenerative scenic walk through nature. You start walking with the guided trail set out by the people before you. Suddenly, you notice the sun shining through a particular gap between two trees. You feel a hunch as you look to the ground, the sun so delicately shines on. You decide to turn off the guided path and into a clear between these trees. You notice this way will be different, and it will ask you to jump over more rocks and climb sharp edges, which will take much more effort than the clear path, you had as an option. You work out the way you feel called to while remaining as safe as possible, progressing through the bush. Regardless of whether you continue to take the guided trail, the clear pathway, or this new way, you are still on a path to somewhere. The direction could be entirely different now. You may end the walk in a completely different place from where you were first deciding to be.

We create our lives by the choices we make from moment to moment. We often forget this because we are habitual; we tend to repeat unconscious patterns. Instead, we could become more conscious of more moments and direct our path in a new direction just by a different choice. Another aspect of choice we need to remember, is for every decision we make, sets out a particular consequence. We simply have consequences for our choices and actions. It's like in NLP, a belief we have is, there is no failure, only feedback. Each option we decide creates a new path in front of us. This means we can completely change the direction and trajectory of our lives simply by one conscious choice. We can always choose again.

3) If we have our own path, we can assume we can either be on it or go off track.
Feeling passionate and being happy is our barometer when seeking our path to living our purpose. This is a key concept Pip McKay incorporated into our Passion and Purpose Coaching Training. We use all our passions throughout our lives to uncover our Archetypes. I love Alicia Keys' song "Girl on Fire" when she belts out, "This girl is on fire, she's walking on fire!" When I hear this, I'm reminded when we are red-hot passionate about something, we are in our zone of genius, we are shining so bright we feel on top of the world; we are on fire. We are passionate when we are on our unique path of contribution and purpose. When we are unmotivated, depressed, and uninspired, we have gone off track and are being signalled to come back home to what lights us up again.

We go off track when we get caught up in drama, focus

on negativity and compete with others. We are on purpose when we live aligned with our heart's priorities (from Chapter Three), focus on what makes us happy and consequently, we naturally live our life of contribution. Remember, the contribution I am referring to could be being the best family member we can be or being a company's CEO – being our happy selves. No matter what we desire, we are contributing to the greater good when we are passionate, regardless of our role. Passion doesn't mean it is always easy and enjoyable. Passion means our heart calls us to pursue this path of interest. There is this deep knowing, it will be worth it.

Ways we go off path from our purpose

We go off path from ourselves and our purpose when we play in drama triangles (explained soon in this Chapter and Chapter Eight), compare ourselves to others and repeat negative patterns with our behaviours. Also, with how we treat others and by self-criticism and judgement (which we went over in Chapter Five with our self-talk). Let's go over some of these now in more detail.

Comparing ourselves to others and being judgemental
We don't find more self-worthiness by perceiving unworthiness in another. Putting others down in our mind, or downplaying others' beauty and capacity in no way, shape or form has us grow more significant. So why do we play this mindset game inside ourselves sometimes? Because there can be parts of us that think, 'If only they were at my level, they would see me for

what I have to go through.' We project our pain and struggle onto others to feel better about how much we are fulfilling our potential – or not. In Australia, we call it "The Tall Poppy Syndrome", which refers to cutting a tall poppy (flower) down to size so that it doesn't stand out higher amongst the rest. It is a term used to describe the culture of criticising, resenting, and undermining the success and ambition of others. Instead of braving our new level of potential and stepping into the space where we are beside those we admire. Our fears and self-defined limitations have us wanting to pull others down so we can feel justified and understood.

If we judge another by what they have achieved, we suggest to our unconscious minds that we can't have those things too. By putting down what we unconsciously deny we want for ourselves, we are pushing these things further away from us – and people. Suppose we are jealous and critical of others' success. In that case, we unconsciously communicate to our body wisdom that if we were to achieve such things, we would feel criticised, judged, and resented by someone. Or we can't believe we can truly get what we want. So rather than be disappointed in ourselves, our unconscious mind stops us from striving for the things we are jealous of. It's a toxic paradox of pushing away the very things we want for ourselves because we can't celebrate success for others.

The moment we start celebrating for others, we are telling our unconscious mind we want this too. We start aligning to the energies of believing we can have it and hence, will more likely create behaviours and emotions in harmony with what we want. I love seeing people have supportive and loving relationships, fantastic health, fun travelling the world, and gorgeous material items such as luxury homes and eco-conscious cars – and I say out loud a lot of the time, to myself, and genuinely mean it, 'Wow, good on them, that looks fun and beautiful.' This feeling allows me to connect with my desires and beliefs that I can find ways to make it happen for myself, too.

Comparing or judging others makes our unconscious mind believe whatever we say about others, we are saying about ourselves. If we want more love, confidence, and beauty in our lives, we need to start noticing, admiring and even genuinely complimenting others when we see it. It still blows my mind how people who are critical of others' successes tend to forget completely the journey and experiences those people must have gone through to achieve what they have. Sure, there is ease in the world where some seem to get things coming to them more easily than others. It can feel painful for life to be so unfair, yet most of the time, it's easy to criticise the everyday person around us as they are more like us than, say, the famous and rich in Hollywood. Hence, the journey of mistakes, struggle, learning, and growth can be entirely dismissed when we only see the end or external result of reward.

If we dismiss the journey of others and are jealous of others' rewards and gifts, we are also dismissing our own experiences and places of genius. We can delete any chance for our own growth and success because we forget our own paths of purpose. People who put down, criticise or are even intimidated by others' successes are deleting and dismissing all the good things in their own life. Consequently, coming away from gratitude, which is the energy of harmonising all the good things coming their way.

We need to understand ourselves, so we do not project our insecurities onto others through jealousy, gaslighting, manipulation or playing a shadow stereotype role. Shadow stereotype roles include playing victim, the overcompensating rescuer of others, the procrastinator, the people pleaser, the saboteur and so on. I go more extensively into these in my coaching and advanced programs. When we find ourselves playing these roles and creating unnecessary and toxic drama. It shows us we are not feeling lovable, good enough or worthy inside ourselves.

If we still feel resentment for our experiences in comparison to others and are holding on to anger, sadness, hurt, guilt, fear, shame, etc., from the past, we continue to project this pain outwards. Commonly this comes out in the form of having negative views on others. Here, healing needs to take place to get back on our ideal path to living our lives of passion and purpose.

Another way we go off path from our purpose is through creating drama by playing in the Drama Triangle.

The Drama Triangle

The Drama Triangle (or Drama Cycle) has become quite well known outside of its original use in psychotherapy and transactional analysis in the context of alcoholics anonymous and the relationship between the alcoholic and their partner. It is a model of dysfunctional social relationships first described in the 1960s by Stephen B. Karpman, M.D. It profoundly illustrates a power game that involves three roles, generally played between two people: Victim, Rescuer and Persecutor.

The Drama Triangle describes how we can play each of

the three roles inside a relationship with anyone in our lives, creating unnecessary conflict, and well… drama! Knowing this model can allow us to become aware of when we are playing in it. Therefore, we can choose differently and come out of the negative cycle.

The Drama Triangle by Stephen B. Karpman, M.D

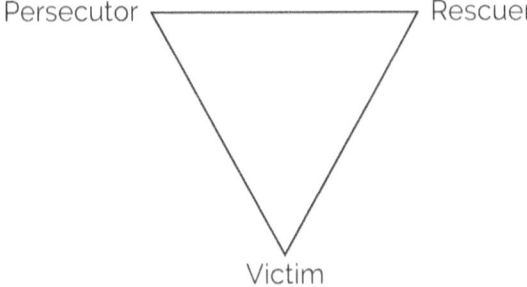

There is now a lot of information out there on this model and we have a powerful coaching process I use both with my clients and in the Evolve Now! Level 1B: Masculine and Feminine Coaching Training created by Pip McKay. Pip created a script and process we use to help people come out of this self-sabotaging and unhealthy pattern we all become addicted to at times in our lives.

What we want to understand here is to become familiar enough with this model so we can notice if we have been caught up in this toxic, life-draining cycle. Knowing how these roles stop us from living our purpose and deciding we don't want to play inside of them anymore.

I teach this model and coach people to come out of them and yet even with this knowledge I have found myself inside

Drama Triangles. It really is a very unpleasant place to live our lives from because they can become all-consuming. Regardless of who we play drama cycles with, the moment we realise it is creating drama and blame games, feeling victim to and a yearning to rescue others, we want to do all we can to relate differently to these people.

The times I have found myself in Drama Triangles since I learned about them, were in forming some new friendships over recent years. There have been two times this has happened, and the interesting thing was how common the structure of the friendships were. Between myself and each of them, not long after getting to know each other, they defaulted to feeling the victim of something they couldn't seem to solve in their lives. I defaulted into wanting to rescue them so they didn't have this problem anymore. They both had done a little work in personal development and because they knew what I did for work, the dynamics of the friendship were blurred. I would sometimes step into my professional skills when they asked for my help. Since they chose to keep holding on to the same problem, all I could do was be their friend instead of their therapist.

I would then make them a persecutor in this relationship because all they could do was talk about the problem and project on to me how I had an easier life than they did. I would then become victim to them, feeling resentment building up that nothing was changing or improving for them. They would also see me as a persecutor when I couldn't just listen to the same problems repeatedly without wanting to see how they could do something about it and feel better. They weren't prepared to feel better so they would also try to rescue me from themselves by giving me advice about my life and how their problems were bigger than mine (their perception of their victimhood was bigger than mine was the general undercurrent of our interactions). They would feel like the victim of the relationship because lo and behold, they still had their same problems and wanted to stay that victim, unconsciously, in their lives. It goes on and on, round and round with each person taking on the different roles at different times.

Just reading this is tiring. Drama is energy-sucking and exhausting. I haven't yet mentioned how I would also talk about my problems in a victimised way so I could relate to them, and they would play the rescuer for me and at some point I am sure I was made persecutor to them because of this. Oh, the drama of it all. This is different to talking about problems with a friend. It is when we see the victim mentality where they hold on to the same problems for secondary gain and significance for a long period of time. Informing the majority of their communication and relationships.

The only way to stop playing in Drama Triangles is to:

1. Become aware of when you are in the cycle.
2. Do all you can to remove yourself from playing each of the roles inside the relationship. The way to end the cycle is to create your life the way you want it to be outside of being a rescuer, victim, or persecutor. This means to stop feeling the victim in the relationship. Stop feeling a need to rescue the other person from their problems. Since the cycle becomes habitual with the way we relate to each other. We stop the cycle by focusing on our own lives of passion, purpose, and contribution. Fill up your days with what makes you happy and the relationship

will unfold and possibly evolve as it will. They will grow with you, or they may not. You will be okay regardless.

Not having a bigger vision for our lives
Another way we can come off our path is not having a higher context as to how we fit in or a bigger vision that goes beyond our own needs, wants and experiences. I spoke about this earlier in the chapter with these four questions for us to contemplate;

- What do you think your "own path" means?
- What do you believe about having your own path to follow?
- What do you believe about destiny?
- What does having a purpose mean to you?

I think there is another question we could ask that goes beyond ourselves and that is:

- Do you feel or believe in something greater than yourself? If so, how would you describe it? (It could be feeling connected to all humanity, to all of nature, to all of earth, to all of consciousness or a God, The Source or whatever it is for you).
    - How does this higher connection support me when I go off path?
    - How can I connect to it more often?

The answers to the above questions are something to carefully consider incorporating into your daily practise. Mine, for example is to read some very special prayers I say to myself at some point in the day. I also consider intentionally thinking about what I am grateful for, and even better, when I write out my gratitude, this is what I call my spiritual practise and it always brings me back home to myself and on my path.

Thinking and living from an old self-identity that is smaller than our goals and dreams - including not believing in self

Of course, we will be off our path from who we are when we let old ways of seeing ourselves run our lives. Over time, our beliefs, values, and experiences create such a strong imprint on who we think we are, we end up having a self-identity which we believe ourselves to be. There is a model from Robert Dilts who contributes to the NLP field, and I'll share this model in Chapter Nine. It describes how our self-identity informs our behaviours and consequently the environment we see around us today.

It is the culmination of beliefs, what we make important in our lives (our values), the environments around us (home, car, office, people, places) that make up how we see ourselves and becomes our self-identity. This self-identity then determines even more of what we believe about ourselves, our values and behaviours. It is not until we choose to change something like our environments, behaviours, beliefs, or values, that we can make a change to the way we view ourselves. They in turn affect each other. Let's look at this more deeply in Chapter Nine. Our self-identity can also be affected by our perceptions of what we think others think of us. This is a result of how those around us speak to us and the influence we take on from others.

How do we get back on path to live a life of passion, purpose and fulfill our potential?

The biggest way we can come back home to ourselves and to living our potential is to know who we are and live from that place of self-perception. It is to implement all the learnings from this book as we connect more deeply with the relationships we have to all areas of our lives.

Here is a summary again of the relationships we have covered and those we are about to cover in the two final chapters of this book:

Self-love is the relationship we have with;

- ♥ how we understand our mind and respect how it works for us,
- ♥ the connection we have to our bodies, which is fundamentally the vehicle which carries our spirit/soul through this physical, human existence, and is our only home,
- ♥ knowing our values, which are the most important priorities in our lives, and we are motivated to fulfil for our hearts to be happy,
- ♥ making self-loving decisions to continually discern what is no longer best versus what we want to have more in our lives, whilst creating beautiful boundaries,
- ♥ paying attention to how we talk to ourselves, which is the way we make judgements and what, in turn, contributes to our behaviours and energy we express in who we are being,
- ♥ listening, acknowledging, and understanding our emotions so we can respect them for the loving messengers they are,

- a bigger picture for our life and feeling connected to something higher than ourselves, feeling supported and guided with a meaning for our lives,
- our relationships with others and the loving communication and personal power we show up to others with,
- appreciating our environment with how it supports us to create a life we love through the actions we take with self-loving, intentional behaviours.

And one final, important relationship to ourselves we need to make sure we connect with and deepen is to our intuition.

Connecting to our intuition
Having intuition allows us to have flow, trust, faith, and love for ourselves and in life. We connect to our intuition when we go beyond our emotions and intellect. Not above or aside of our emotions and intellect but *beyond them*. This means that both have been listened to first. Do this by writing down how you feel about a particular event or topic and then write down all of your logic and thoughts about it. After this, be willing to be open to your inner intelligence and listen to the voice that knows what is best for you.

Your intuition always speaks to you as a calm and wise voice. It is never erratic, aggressive, or cocky. Your intuition can come through as a whisper or a confident voice of yours and it will always be calm and certain. Our mind (intellect) and heart (emotions) will sometimes not like the answer it gives us. If we are willing to surrender these for our inner knowing to come through, we must be willing to pay attention, regardless of how we feel or think about its wisdom. Surrendering means to let go of fear and the attachment to having the answer make complete sense. When you know, you know. Follow it.

There are two main reasons we can't hear our intuition and they are:

1. **Because our intellect is getting in the way – yet it is not actually logical, we are just attached to a particular outcome.** Our thoughts steer us into believing a certain logic makes sense when it doesn't.

   An example of this is thinking that by moving to a cheaper area to live in, moving homes will create a significantly better financial position. This logic is not always true because there are many other factors to consider such as selling and moving expenses, possibly lower wages in the new area, now less equity in the new property and lower investment potential in the future if no further investment of money is made.

   Being attached to an outcome with our mind, can have us delete other important factors in the decision-making process. Usually there are deeper emotional reasons striving to be fulfilled and if they are not acknowledged, the intellect without intuition can lead to poor decision making.

2. **Because our emotions are getting in the way, particularly fear.** Fear can be a big block to hearing our intuition because the purpose of fear is to protect us. We feel if we have a fear then we must be right in thinking it is going to happen – because feeling safe is on the line. If we are attached to a particular outcome with strong

feelings towards that outcome, they will get in the way of us hearing the part of us that already likely knows the answer.

Once we get out of our intuition's way by surrendering our thoughts and emotions about the situation or topic, we can connect and listen to our wise inner guide. **Our intuition can speak to us through a vision, a gut feeling from our body, or we hear it like a voice speaking to us.** Follow it. Your intuition has your highest interests at heart. I know I am on a journey to deepen this connection with my intuition. You will benefit from connecting with yours more deeply and often too.

Follow your inspiration

This chapter is about connecting to a higher wisdom than ourselves. A most important way we can do this is to be in our inspiration. If we look at the word, we can break it up to be: in-spirit. We are inspired when we are connected to our spirit – the source – whatever it is for you. Here is a piece I wrote on inspiration a few years ago:

INSPIRATION.

It's where all energy begins and from infinite possibilities, one idea that touches your heart and ignites your spirit starts to come into form. You feel a calling to pull it down from the ether and to experience it through all your senses.

It may be seeing someone doing magical things in helping others and you are deeply moved and reminded that you have the same capacity to also bring magic and love to this world.

It may be a song and you feel a connection with its vibration, words and/or the melody. Motivated, you just enjoy the creation of it, knowing it came from the same source that you are also connected to. In the minutes of this experience you deeply realise the present is all that matters, having you let go of your illusions of stress and your only focus becomes to move your body to the beat.

It could be a child who reminds you how loved you are as they say something so profound back to you, that you smile, knowing they learned it through your influence and yet they have their own brilliant mind all at the same time. What else is more important than to see a child who knows they are loved, love you back whilst showing you their unique imprint in this world?

These examples to me and anything that brings you INSPIRATION are the essences of bringing us back to our joy for life.

To release us from darkness, stagnation and hopelessness, it is when we find a spark of true inspiration bringing us back to our passion and purpose.

And so the journey at least begins here, bringing us ever closer to a life of passion, purpose, contribution and self-actualisation. It's the great start we take... moving us into our next step of focusing on bringing that inspiration down into our reality and fulfilling more of our potential.

Conclusion of this vow

I vow to honour my own path and to trust in the big picture of my life.

I honour the relationship I have with a higher connection to myself.

Whatever you believe in, whether it's something bigger than you or simply feeling a part of a community, a part of humanity, a part of earth or anything else which reminds you there is a bigger picture beyond yourself. Let it help you connect with a deeper meaning to your life. When we have a deeper meaning, it can be the horizon for us, that no matter what is going on in our lives, there is always the steady and certain knowing there is a beautiful horizon which connects everything together.

Notice what lights you up, inspires your heart and gives your tummy butterflies of excitement. Follow this as much as you can.

A summary of what you learned in

Chapter Seven

♥

I vow to honour my own path and to trust in the big picture of my life.

I honour the relationship I have with a higher connection to myself.

- ♥ Lauren's story on meeting herself by finding her Passion & Purpose Archetypes
- ♥ Our relationship to living our daily lives by contributing to the bigger picture of who we came here to be
- ♥ Our authentic archetypal energies
- ♥ There are many paths to our passions and purpose
- ♥ What does it mean to honour our own path?
- ♥ Ways we go off path from our purpose
- ♥ How do we get back on path to live a life of passion, purpose and fulfill our potential?
- ♥ Follow your inspiration

Devoting yourself to applying the learnings in this chapter:

1. Using the Self-Loving Resource of Environment: Use the resource of the external world and the environment that surrounds you to connect with your inspiration.

2. Using the Self-Loving Resource of Tools: Grab your journal or use the free course I created for you at www.laurenjobson.com/bookfreecourse where you can create a vision board to draw down from your inspiration.

Also, use a tool to help connect with your gratitude and perhaps, a prayer practise. I have a gratitude journal and I also have my prayers printed out so I can read them easily every day.

In my free self-love planner you can access at the link above, there are spaces for vision boarding, goal setting and daily gratitude.

3. Using the Self-Loving Resource of Intuition: This is our wise, calm inner voice. It is our gut and body wisdom, our inner mentor to trust and follow. We all need to learn how to listen to our intuition more often and deepen our relationship with this inner wise one. Our intuition is our most profound and most trustworthy resource. We spoke about how to connect with it in this chapter.

4. Using the Self-Loving Resource of Action: All the information in this chapter could just be interesting theory until we devote ourselves to taking applied action. Grab your gratitude journal, use my free self-love planner, or create one today.

Chapter Eight

I Vow to Take Ownership in My Relationships.

I honour the relationship I have with self-loving boundaries and communication.

Vow Eight

"A life built on deep healing, growth and flow is a series of rebirthings. We must each learn to be the midwives for our own rebirthing processes, to remember we are in a bifurcation process and to assist us in moving through it with as much grace as possible. Better yet, we base our most intimate relationships with one or more people to successfully master this dynamic of nature, while bringing in more and more life-supporting energy into our energy fields."

GENE LATIMER

I was blessed to have fallen in love with an amazing man, Brendon, when I was seventeen, and we've been together ever since. We have been married for ten years and have two daughters together. Before our first baby we had our fur child, our beloved puppy dog.

It is close to a fairy tale, and I am so grateful for our relationship. Of course, it hasn't always been amazing. Earlier in our time dating, we parted ways because I had unconsciously and energetically pushed him away. This was to reveal itself as a pattern of mine.

The first time my pattern played out was when my first boyfriend told me that he didn't know why, but felt he had to break up with me after about a year of being with him. It was shocking and heartbreaking. The relationship had gone well up until this point. There were no apparent problems. It was loving, supportive, fun, and loyal. He mentioned feelings of not deserving me and said he wasn't sure if he loved me anymore. These words were to be repeated, and this sudden break up pattern happened again with the two following partners, one of those being my husband today, Brendon.

It was another exciting evening when Brendon, after ten months of dating, visited me at my parent's house. We were only eighteen and nineteen, and I can still hear, to this day, how my parent's greeted him happily at the door. All was well when he arrived. We had already shared many amazing experiences over the ten months, including my eighteenth birthday, my drumming concerts, my high school final exams, graduating High School as School Captain, and starting college to get into the music industry. He was in the first and second year of his apprenticeship with the company he still works for today.

We were happy and in love. But this night, those words I was to hear again; 'I don't know why but I feel I need to break up with you.' In utter disbelief and shock, I kept asking why and he couldn't answer me clearly. When I walked him to his car, and we said goodbye, I asked him if he didn't love me anymore, and he couldn't even answer this for me. I was crushed and confused again. But this time, I felt I had lost the man I wanted to grow old with.

I retreated into myself and was lucky to have beautiful support and love from my dearest friends and family. My bestie arranged for flowers to be sent to me since she couldn't be with me physically. She lived in North Queensland with her love. My loved ones knew how hard this time was for me.

One day not long after the breakup, my mum told me my Uncle Simon had called her and asked if I would be interested in attending his first weekend workshop. I wasn't given much information, except it was his first workshop after becoming something called, an NLP Trainer. I had no idea what NLP was, but I knew he was studying mindset stuff. I thought, why not? After my first encounter with overcoming my stomach aches, I loved pulling books off his shelf at family get togethers such as books by Louise L. Hay, Deepak Chopra, Wayne Dyer so I knew I loved this personal development stuff he was into. I would be supporting him whilst exploring my curiosity and openness to anything which might help me. I had little awareness of how that workshop would ultimately affect the trajectory of my career and life today.

Simon's workshop started on a Friday evening and continued over the weekend. On the first night, we were given a piece of wood and were told we might have a breakthrough. Simon directed us to pick an area of our life we most wanted to improve. I chose intimate relationships. We then needed to write on one side of the wood everything we wanted in this area of our life. I started to write down all of the feelings and attributes I wanted in my ideal relationship. It didn't take long for a deep sadness to arise in my body, and I cried and cried and cried. Everything I had written down, I'd had all those things with Brendon.

I was almost inconsolable and had to leave the room so I could continue to cry in my own space. Simon's lovely assistant, Suzie, came out to be with me. When she saw I was ready to listen, she brought my attention to the two plants in each corner of the room. They were across from each other. She told me a metaphor, which I recognised many years later when I saw it on a slide in a training I was teaching. I realised that she had heard it from none other than Pip McKay. I love to this day how things come around. How we can see the connections and ripple effects we all have on each other, like people we were destined to meet and stories we were meant to hear.

The metaphor was about how the two plants each had their own pot. They each grew beautifully in their unique pot with how they were watered, their soil and their overall environment. They had to be rooted in their own pot to thrive. Suzie had me imagine; if these two plants connected, what would happen if one plant came out of its pot and started to depend on the other's roots for its own growth and sustainability of life? She told me, since I was still in no state to confidently reply, how eventually, the plant that came out of their pot would literally suck the life out of the pot they depended on. Can a plant not rooted in its own soil, sustained by someone else's life, grow healthily or ever thrive to fulfil its potential? Now, here is my retelling of this twenty years later. It is my version of what Suzie shared with me at the time. I found it a little confusing why I was being told this seemingly random story about silly plants. But it changed my state from despair and sadness and we wrapped up the workshop for the evening.

On the following day of the workshop, we wrote down our values (like we had on the board of wood the night before) for all the things that were important to us in that area of life. Then, working with another participant, we asked each other questions from a script we were given to bring out any limiting beliefs we had.

I answered one question with the words, 'I can't be happy

without a boyfriend.' Wow, what a limiting belief that was, because I could see how this would create an unhealthy dependency on someone else for my own happiness. Perhaps the story about the plants from the night before was more relevant than I thought. It became clearer how I could have unconsciously been pushing my boyfriends away because the pressure was too much for them. They, too, were unaware of what they were feeling, and unable to really explain the reason for breaking up with me. Very likely, they felt the energy of supporting and providing for my happiness was laying a heavy weight on their shoulders.

The final thing we did, was learn a process we could do with our incredible unconscious minds to let go of and resolve limiting beliefs. Thanks to the previous day's exercise, we had become conscious of the beliefs holding us back and sabotaging our desires. Once resolved, I could instead feel whole and happy inside myself, regardless of whether I had a boyfriend or not.

I vividly remember how I felt by the end of the weekend training - even the details of what I was wearing, a green and white striped cotton skirt and top, because it had profoundly changed my life. It was the beginning of my interest in and love of NLP. It is the reason I chose to pursue NLP as my modality of personal development. Perhaps even more importantly, I could make the changes inside myself, without having to tell anyone anything of what I learned or had done. I was able to attract Brendon back into my life by letting the events unfold naturally. He and I reconnected and organised to go out and have a conversation about where we were both at in life, just a few months after our breakup. There was this magnetism back to each other, I believe, because my energy was different since resolving my old belief. We recommitted to each other that night. He has always felt like the love of my life. I fall in love with him at more profound levels still, eighteen years on.

With this self-awareness and by taking responsibility to make changes in my life, I experienced an example of how our inner world completely affects our external reality. More specifically, how our intimate partner is a direct reflection to us of our personal "stuff" and how they, more than anyone, play out our unresolved issues in order to learn and grow.

Our relationship with others - our outside world reflects our inner world

We are the creators of our reality because we simply can't notice anything outside of us that isn't inside us on some level. We cannot notice a quality in another person unless, to some degree, we have that quality ourselves or even have the capability of tapping into that quality. Such as being selfish, judgemental, and mean – frankly, anything we notice in another, we can only see because we have this to some degree inside of ourselves too.

Carl Jung, the founder of analytical psychology, said, "everything that irritates us about others can lead us to an understanding of ourselves." He also described that the more we have a problem with someone, the more it's likely a reflection of us. It is more complex than saying we are exactly like the person we dislike, but it's closer to what we don't like to feel comfortable admitting too. This is a confronting concept and I'll explain more detail soon.

How do we make meaning of the outside world and create differing realities?

The diagram below shows us (again, as also shown in Chapter One) a model from NLP and it's my absolute favourite model for understanding how we work as human beings and why we do what we do.

The NLP Communication Model

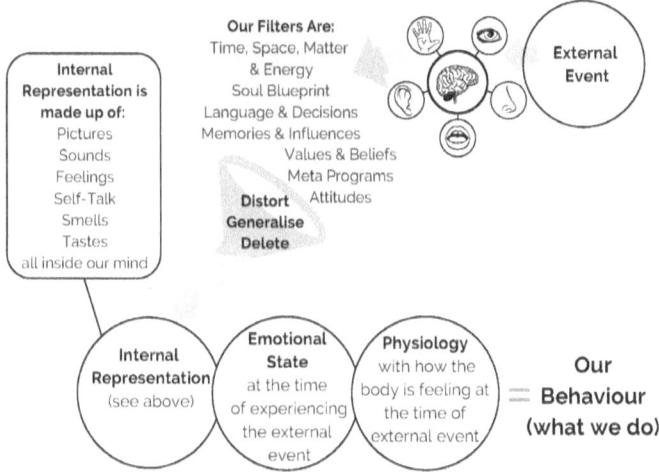

I want to refer to the NLP Communication Model here to understand how our outside world is truly a reflection of our inner world. This also explains how we create our realities.

Reality is what feels true to us. It is interesting to note we describe reality as being real when in fact, we all have different realities between us. Let's see how this model shows us this and what it means for how we create meaning in our lives. We will then explore how we connect and communicate in our relationships according to our differing realities.

As mentioned in Chapter One, and it bears repeating; we process our external world through our five senses; we touch/feel, see, hear, taste, and smell. It is then, according to what event we are processing in each moment, that we filter this information as we delete, distort and generalise according to our memories, values, beliefs, attitudes, personality types (meta programs), environment and even the language we speak. It also includes our soul blueprint which I have added to this model.

With the concept of how our external world reflects our inner world, here is an example of how these deletions, distortions, and generalisations work. Someone who has lost faith in having a successful intimate relationship will most likely delete a lot of opportunities to meet someone special because, in their mind, it is too painful and risky to go there. They make generalisations, which is another word for stereotypes, about people they could date. Meaning they dismiss many potential partners due to past bad experiences. For this person, their unconscious mind seemingly protects them from getting hurt again because it wants the best for them. Yet, the irony of emotional logic is that protection is limiting the person from ever getting what they want if they continue to function from this place of preventing pain.

Since we are making meaning of our outside world all the

time, according to our memories, values, beliefs, attitudes, personality types, environment and even the language we speak, we can now talk about how it is we can only perceive in others what we have at some level, inside of us.

Our relationships are our mirrors of ourselves. Our most intimate relationships reflect our most significant places of growth

Our partner, more than anyone else in our lives, even if we have children, confronts us with all our unresolved "stuff" and reflects it back to us. This is because we get to choose our intimate partner, and they are the one person we are generally most vulnerable with. It is with them we share all of who we are. Since they see us naked, not just physically, but in our most raw and real moments emotionally, mentally, and spiritually.

The interesting thing about how our relationships are a mirror is how they show us our places of growth. We call this idea, perception is projection. It is when we are triggered, meaning something occurs outside of us and we feel a negative emotion in our body as a sensation. It is in these moments where we generally default to blame the person who "made us" feel that way. This concept shows us that we need to look inside and notice the root cause of our triggers.

Before we move on, it is important we know the difference between how we would like to and deserve to be treated. The level of respect we expect as a minimum standard for ourselves, versus looking inwards to take responsibility for a trigger we have from someone else's behaviour. In learning perception is projection, we must consider that it is *not* about blaming someone else's negative and bad behaviours on ourselves. When I write about being triggered by someone else meaning that we should look within us, I am not saying that every problem we have with the other person means we need to just change ourselves. Instead, the looking inwards side of it when triggered by someone else's mistreatment or bad behaviour means to have enough self-awareness and self-respect to do something about it resourcefully (with respect and being mindful of all the consequences). I will share a few tips on creating boundaries with effective communication later in this chapter.

Perception is projection

This is a concept I have been teaching for the last fifteen years. It is so profound that many who learn it find more and more ways to understand and implement it into their lives effectively. Even after teaching it thousands of times over myself, I still get new insights. If you truly grasp this, it is revolutionary to our self-image, self-esteem, and self-love. Perception is projection is essential to learn as it is all about how our inner world projects out onto our external world and vice versa. It explains how our masculine outward projection of how we see and experience the world directly reflects our feminine inner world of perceptions. Hence, another concept of our Sacred Marriage within.

Here is a diagram below that explains the concept and another to show an example:

Perception is Projection Explanation Diagram

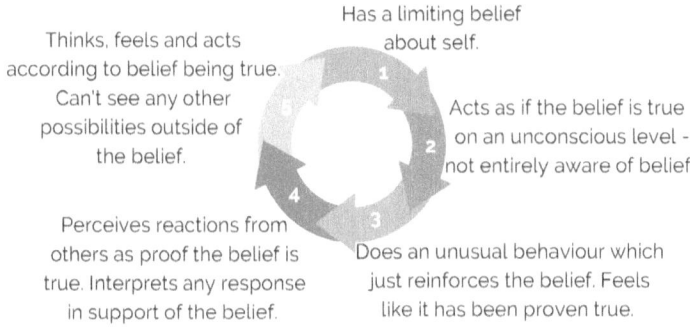

Perception is Projection Example Diagram

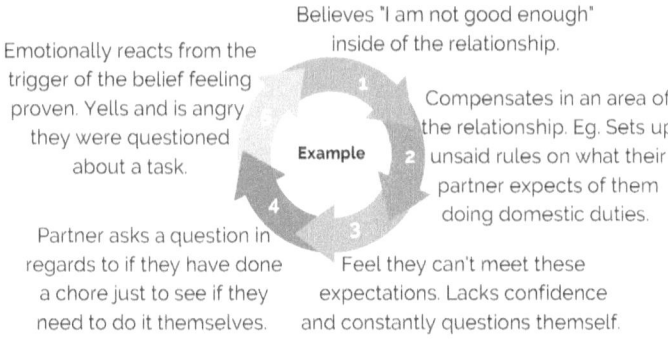

Here is another example of how this can play out:

1. Someone with low self-esteem has a belief like they are not good enough, and their self-talk could be along the lines of, 'What if people see through me and realise I am

no good, too?' Because of these emotions, beliefs and self -talk playing in their mind they...
2. Say things out loud to others like, 'I know you might think I already have these skills because of what I do for work, but I am still learning.' This makes them feel they need to ask permission from others to make mistakes (no one needs permission, we are all learning, and all make mistakes).
3. This person then judges themselves and questions every move they make. They are likelier to make mistakes and do behaviours they wouldn't normally do when not feeling pressured.
4. They perceive any feedback from others as condescending or think they are being told they have made a mistake. No matter how someone says something to them, they expect the feedback to prove that not only are they not good enough at the task but also innately not good enough as a person.
5. They perceive the responses from others reinforce their belief, which means it cycles through again until the belief (their perception) is changed.

Step 1 is an inner perception about self.

Steps 2 and 3 are outwards projections of Step 1.

Steps 4 and 5 are then reinforced self-perceptions from Steps 2 and 3.

Change needs to happen at Step 1 where the belief about self is different and positive. Creating different projections and perceptions moving forward.

Here is an example of how making a fundamental belief

change at Step 1, changes the projections and perceptions for this person going forward:

1. Someone believes they are good enough innately with who they are and that it is okay to make mistakes because they know life is all about learning.
2. They are present in their interactions because they are no longer second-guessing their every move and don't need permission or approval from others around them. They care what others think in balance with what they think of themselves, so they are open to feedback.
3. They are present in their actions because they know their worthiness and lovableness has nothing to do with whether they are successful or not. They give their best efforts to the tasks for the day and are open to learning with self-reflection and feedback from others. They show up as themselves and practice confidence and self-assurance.
4. They no longer feel a need to compensate or to defend themselves with the feedback they receive or from the results of their actions. They know they are good enough regardless of anything. Receiving feedback from others is a gift because they can see it as further growth and learning with what they choose to implement.
5. They have humility through being able to laugh at themselves or apologise appropriately if they have made a mistake. They can genuinely thank those who have given them feedback and show themselves willing to do better next time. This reinforces their belief they are good enough with who they are. They now only feel more

pride and love for themselves, that they can be a better version of their potential moving forward.

In our training, we go over all the ways we can perceive in others what we need to learn from and resolve in ourselves. I've seen this concept be taught in the field of NLP as "Perception is projection means everything you have a problem with in others, is you!" and the Trainer has left it at that. Let us discern and be clear on this. Not everything we don't like in others reflects something we need to heal from. What do we then say about when we see aggression and violence in other people? If we get triggered by aggression, how does it mean it is true for us, too? I know for a fact most of my students who come and learn NLP, plus a lot of people who are triggered by aggression and violence are not aggressive or violent themselves. The truth is, it's a bit more complex than that.

I use the example of the Zen story of two monks and a woman. The story goes that there are two monks who have taken a vow to not touch women and they go for a long walk and come to a river they need to cross. They see a woman who is stuck as she can't get across the river without help. One monk offers his help and decides he needs to carry her over his shoulders to get her across. They continue walking and hours pass. The other monk tried his best not to question it but he couldn't keep it in any longer so he blurted out "I can't believe you picked up that woman when we vowed not to ever touch a woman!" The monk replies, "Brother, I put her down many hours ago, why are you still carrying her?"

It is when we carry things for too long it shows a trigger we need to learn from. We can all hate war, violence, and crime without being criminals ourselves. It is when we are carrying the emotion and energy of something we have seen in our outside world that is most likely something we need to run through our perception is projection check, to discern what is it inside of us that is triggering us, and that we need to heal. It's one of the most humbling places to take responsibility for our projections. We need to let go of our ego and embrace our humility in order to see our part in creating our perceptions.

There are some layers to perception is projection that can be deleted in its teaching. Let me go through them now. There are four types of perception is projection (P is P) that Pip McKay taught me:

1) Direct

This is the simple way P is P is taught and explained that the very thing you have a problem with in another is the very trait or behaviour you have in yourself.

An example of this is when a person is complaining about someone being a gossiper whilst they themselves gossip behind other people's backs. This is a direct example because it is the same behaviour. They are indulging in the habit which they are complaining of. It is like a mirror is being held up for them to see how they are doing it themselves.

Other examples are perceiving others to be selfish when one is selfish too. Or getting angry at "bad drivers" when they are not a good driver themselves. Accusing others of loving drama when they indeed are causing a lot of the drama themselves. The list can go on.

2) Back on self

This is when someone has a problem with something they don't do directly to others, but they do it in a slightly different way back on themselves.

An example of this is noticing and being triggered by others being aggressive and mean. This can be a P is P issue with the person being aggressive and mean towards themselves with their self-talk or sabotaging behaviours.

3) Metaphoric or symbolic

This is when it is symbolic between two different behaviours, because the true problem is shown through a metaphor.

For example, someone who has a problem with back seat drivers, yet when she is a passenger in a car, she doesn't back seat drive, just allows the driver to be in control of the car. So how is this P is P, when she really gets triggered by others telling her what to do when she is driving? Well, turns out, she was going to coaching because she micromanages her staff which caused a lot of problems in her business. It was a control issue. She was acting like a back seat driver to her staff by over-controlling them when she could have just trusted them to be in the driver's seat of their role.

4) Denied Self

This is when someone is triggered by what someone else has or has achieved because they deny they want it for themselves.

This has been mentioned in the previous chapter when I said, 'If we ever judge another by what they have or have achieved, we are suggesting to our unconscious minds that we can't have those things ourselves.' By the very process of putting something down, we unconsciously deny we want it for ourselves. Someone could say something like, 'Why would anyone spend so much money on a luxury car like that? It's ridiculous!' With this negative energy around it, this shows a projection that it's a perception they don't believe they can afford it themselves. So they deny they want it, too, in order to not get disappointed.

What happens when we make change within ourselves, how does it change the projection I had?
When we notice any of the four ways we can do 'perception is projection', it then shows us what needs healing inside of us. Once we make this change, a few things can happen as a result. This is also what happens once we do a negative influence clearing process and resolve negative emotions and limiting beliefs from our past.

The thing we were triggered about;

- ♥ is the same but we are no longer triggered or even notice it
or
- ♥ the person who triggered us miraculously changes because of the change we have made inside ourselves
or
- ♥ the person who triggered us is naturally let go from our lives by a series of unfolding events that work win/win for all involved.

I've been continually humbled and in awe of the many times my students and clients have done the process of Matrix Therapies® Clearing Negative Influence process, and how just by beautiful synchronicity, the person whose influence they cleared is in touch with them. One example was when a student hadn't spoken to her father often, especially since she moved overseas. She had a lot of emotion around not getting the love and support she wanted growing up. She did the process on his influence, (of course she didn't tell him as that is not necessary in this work) and he sent her a text that night saying, 'I don't tell you enough that I love you.' Magic!

Another example was when a student of mine was having some trouble with his connection between his teenage daughters since his divorce with their mum. He felt they were angry with him and he didn't know how he could reconnect with them. After he had done the clearing process with his ex-wife, again, not telling anyone, he received a text message that night from one of his daughters saying, 'Love you Dad.' Miraculous and magical.

One of my all-time favourite client results was a teenage boy who started to miss out on so much school, he was on his last warning for being dismissed. He came to me open hearted as we cleared the influence of his alcoholic father. Out poured all his inner wisdom and his processing was beautiful to witness. Without any change in the consistent, loving support of his mother, through his own free will, he went back to school and the thought of graduating became an easy achievement for him. He graduated and is now working, being a responsible adult, continually working on himself and getting support when he needs it. What a man!

How do we lovingly communicate our boundaries and only allow what is good for us?

Have you let anyone cross the boundaries that make you feel small, unseen and not understood? If you have any of these types of relationships, then it is time to put yourself first and surround yourself with those who lift you higher, remind you of your brightest light and see you for all your magic and beauty. There may be some relationships in your life that are not like this, and at the same time, you feel you can't cut them out of your life completely.

A gentle reminder to check over your relationships to see if you are playing in any Drama Triangles which we covered in Chapter Seven. If you find there is a habitual pattern of feeling like the dynamics of a relationship is feeling victim to or rescuing in the hope that if they can be rescued from their own victimhood, then maybe they could love and treat you in the way you crave. Or perhaps you are being made a persecutor. This is a Drama Triangle and it will only get more dramatic and toxic if no change to the role playing is made.

Here are some things you can do instead;

1. When you are communicating with this unresourceful person, see yourself surrounded by a bubble of light and love connected to your higher self and imagine that all the negative energy that affects you is now bouncing off your bubble and returning into the light.
2. Realise that this person's negativity is not actually about you. It will be about what they have experienced in life, with the lack of resources they have. Their pain is projected on to you. Know this and practice the above, and if you feel this person influences you too much, then it might be worth doing a Matrix Therapies® process to cut the cords from this energy. This is a process we do which can allow the best and most wanted outcome to happen

which is either the relationship naturally changes or leaves your life resourcefully. Or if it is someone who you still want to have a relationship with, it deepens the connection as it's like relating to them with a fresh start.

The Agreement Communication Frame – respectful language to help overcome resistance and create boundaries

Here is a helpful way we can communicate our boundaries respectfully. It is also helpful for important communication with tricky situations such as dealing with complaints, when you have a controversial view to others or are trying to overcome resistance in another. It is called the agreement frame from NLP.

The first thing we must remember in this context is to not use the words "but" or "however" as they negate everything you said before those words. They can be used effectively such as 'You didn't get the result you wanted **but** you gave it a go and that's what matters.' When you are first becoming conscious of a lot of unconscious, habitual language in everyday life, it's easier if you focus on taking out the words completely. Once you know you can use these words intentionally, bring them back in.

We want to replace the words "but" and "however" with the word "and".

"And" is such a magical, inclusive word and sits with the listener and receiver of the communication. It is much more comfortable than the negations of "but" and "however".

I also encourage you not to use the word "understand"

particularly when people have a complaint. When we say "I understand" in most instances, people feel no one could possibly understand all that they have been through and the entire context surrounding it.

Let's see this in action with the agreement frame I use a lot.

The Agreement Frame

The agreement frame is mostly made up of three options but then we can mix it up too, see below:

1. **I agree with you and** __(your extra point or bringing them back to the main point)_____.
2. **I respect what you are saying and** _____.
3. **I appreciate what you are saying** (can identify a positive intent of theirs) **and** _____.

Examples could be:

1. **I agree** it is not an easy thing to do at first **and** let's go through this together step by step.
2. **I respect** your thinking with this as it's really great to explore all the options we have **and** we need to consider x, y, z too.
3. **I appreciate** your point of view and being vulnerable to share that here **and** these are the reasons x, y z we need to look at other options.

1. Agree – use only if you do agree.
2. Respect
3. Appreciate

You could also say:
I hear what you are saying **and**...
I see what you are saying **and**...
I feel what you mean **and**...

Read all the above out loud. Read them while substituting "and" to "but" or "however" and notice how it is not as conducive to open communication and overcoming resistance – it actually creates more of it.

Just use lovely, magical "ands" and an option from the agreement frames above instead. You may not find it easy at first to take out your "buts, however and understand" and you will find it easier and more natural the more you do it.

Why receptivity is not only self-loving but most loving to others, too.

When we close ourselves off from receiving all sorts of things - whether a compliment, a gift, or money in exchange for a service we provide, we stop the giver from receiving too, and no one wins.

It can be common for us along our path of learning to love ourselves, to shut down our ability to receive, due to feelings of lack of worthiness, feeling unlovable, or simply wanting to please people and only give to others. Because, in actual truth, to receive is to be vulnerable and to be the person who isn't in control at that moment. You see, the giver is in control of the situation because they know what they are giving, when they will give, and the reason behind the gift. The receiver is the one who relinquishes even a moment of control to the giver. It can be much easier for someone to feel like they can just give their entire lives, when really what is happening is they are protecting the parts of them that would be seen if they were able to receive what they want, fully.

Suppose we were to believe that we are spiritual beings having a physical experience as human beings. In that case, we could believe we are here to experience and enjoy all the richness of living in such a physical world of possibilities. Do we taste enough goodness? Do we grasp enough goodness with our physical hands and our heart? Do we open ourselves up wide enough to be fully seen and be rewarded in return by allowing us to receive our deepest desires? To me, this is the journey of self-love. It is receiving all of life and permitting ourselves, from ourselves only, to love ourselves enough to ask for what we want. By being vulnerable enough with all our insecurities, doubts, fears and any other darkness, we are able to call in more light.

Conclusion of this vow

I vow to take ownership in my relationships.
I honour the relationships I have with self-loving boundaries and communication.

I absolutely love the quote I opened this chapter with:

"*A life built on deep healing, growth and flow is a series of rebirthings. We must each learn to be the midwives for our own rebirthing processes, to remember that we are in a bifurcation process and to assist us in moving through it with as much grace as possible. Better yet, we base our most intimate relationships with one or more people to successfully master this dynamic of nature, while bringing in more and more life-supporting energy into our energy fields."* – Gene Latimer

The above quote I used from my NLP Master Practitioner manual where we go over the concept of bifurcation points (pronounced bye-fur-kay-tion) which is just a technical name for getting to the point of built-up energy where new solutions and ways of being are needed. It's a split, a branching out, a fork in the road. Bifurcation points are when we are coming out of our old and known boxes of being and are in the middle before a new place of breakthrough. It can be when we need to have a difficult conversation, a place of conflict or resistance or just a new place of honesty and depth in a relationship. Relationships ask us to grow in ways we don't realise since we constantly give and receive energy from others, being influenced and influencing. In time, the closer we get to someone, the more energy investment there is. To know someone is to find times when there is a bifurcation point. A place where there is a choice – a new order or level of depth to the relationship or a place where it could fall away or significantly change in some way. To deeply connect with others is to face bifurcation points where communication determines where the relationship could go. The critical question is: are we willing to take responsibility for our self-perceptions and communicate with self-agency?

I can personally vouch that this could be one of the hardest things we do as human beings; to connect so deeply with others that we find times when we are invited to be incredibly vulnerable with the accompanying risk of getting hurt. Our only bridge to each other is through our communication. The only way we can resolve conflict and create deeper, more meaningful relationships is to be in the uncomfortable place of bifurcation points. To be at this point of intimacy with another means choosing to find ways to communicate with patience, listening skills and empathy whilst also taking personal responsibility for our perceptions and actions.

It's not easy. We don't always get it right in communicating when we feel intensely emotional about something. But I know for sure that it is the only thing worth getting hurt for - finding the right people to love and trust and continuously working on deepening the connection.

I am grateful to have people who love and forgive me when I haven't communicated as effectively or as lovingly as I would expect from myself. Again, it is a process. We are all in process, and we love and learn.

A summary of what you learned in

Chapter Eight

**I vow to take ownership in my relationships.
I honour the relationships I have with
self-loving boundaries and communication.**

- Lauren's story about boyfriends breaking up with her
- Our relationship with others - our outside world reflects our inner world
- How do we make meaning of the outside world and create differing realities?
- Our relationships are our mirrors of ourselves. Our most intimate relationships reflect our most significant places of growth
- Four types of perception is projection
- What happens when we make change within ourselves, how does it change the projection?
- How do we lovingly communicate our boundaries and only allow what is good for us?
- The Agreement Frame
- Why receptivity is not only self-loving but most loving to others, too.

Devoting yourself to applying the learnings in this chapter:

1. Using the Self-Loving Resource of Tools: Grab your journal or use the free course I created for you at www.laurenjobson.com/bookfreecourse where you can answer the questions below and more, online.

Let's explore our own 'perception is projection' examples:

Write down some triggers you have in relationships such as selfishness, criticism, feeling put down, ignored, etc., and then look at how you might do these yourself. What changes do you need to make inside of yourself and what communication or change of behaviour needs to happen?

2. Using the Self-Loving Resource of Support: A Matrix Therapies® and NLP Master Practitioner can help you remove any blocks, such as limiting beliefs and emotions you might have become aware of from this chapter. The first thing a Master Practitioner will encourage, is to do negative influence clearing of others and then to resolve the emotional gestalts of the umbrella emotions and any other emotions you may still be holding on to from the past.

Since NLP is all about understanding self, others and communication, if relationships and communicating more effectively are important for you to improve, access my

NLP Training online or face to face. Get in touch with me to learn more about NLP. I offer a free recorded NLP Masterclass you can access too at https://www.laurenjobson.com/nlp-masterclass-access

3. Using the Self-Loving Resource of Forgiveness: This is a reminder that life and self-love is a process of learning. Do what you feel drawn to and practise forgiveness. Particularly self-forgiveness. I also like EFT (emotional freedom technique) for forgiveness as the script is beautiful: "Even though I (state problem), I deeply and completely, love and accept myself". I will share resources on how to do this in my online course. Again, doing Matrix Therapies® is also wonderful for the practise of forgiveness.

Chapter Nine

I Vow to Take Action with Supportive and Intentional Behaviours.

I honour the relationship I have with my external world and how I show up in It.

Vow Nine

> *"You will never have a greater or lesser dominion than that over yourself... the height of a man's success is gauged by his self-mastery; the depth of his failure by his self-abandonment..."*
>
> LEONARDO DA VINCI

In my twenties, I couldn't see myself ever being in touch with my older sisters because I thought if they wanted to find me and connect, somehow, they would have surely found a way by now. Since meeting and learning about some of my other siblings I didn't grow up with, my experiences had me feeling cautious of not wanting to rock my sister's worlds by getting in touch. In case they didn't want me to. On one of my trips to England in my early twenties, my Uncle Simon had found my sisters' profiles on Facebook and sent them to me. He said I could be in touch with them if I wanted because here was a way I could. I was hurt from previous experience and hadn't yet resolved the pain with another sibling I had met in my teen years. So I took a look at their profiles, noticed how much they looked like me, and left it at that.

A couple of years later, whilst I was doing some of my wedding preparation, I put on a TV show that was all about family reunions. There was this episode about two women in their seventies who had just found out they were twins. They had been separated at birth and could meet each other if they wanted. As I watched them meet each other, they embraced and cried their eyes out. These twins felt overjoyed to have found each other, like a part of themselves they didn't realise was missing was now found. I knew in that moment I didn't want to be in my seventies, getting in touch with my sisters and wishing I had done it earlier. So, after a few days of building up my courage, I jumped on my computer, opened Facebook, went to my sisters' profiles, and messaged them this:

27th February 2012, 6.26 pm Sydney time. I was 25 years old.

> *"Hi Louise and Lisa, I'm so sorry if this comes as a big shock and an unwanted one. I was watching a show the other day on reuniting family members, and it really inspired me to get in touch with you. Do you remember me at all? I thought it might be nice for us to just be in touch on here and make a connection even if it's brief.* ☺ *I'd love to hear from you and get to know you.* ☺
>
> *Love Lauren (Lauren Lett on my birth certificate) xx"*

My oldest sister, Lisa, who was eight years old when we had to say goodbye, after reading my message above, fell down to her knees and cried saying, 'My baby sister has finally found me.'

I heard from both of them saying they were very happy I messaged them. They also mentioned they had spoken of Mum and I often whilst growing up.

My two older sisters are truly incredible people. I have had the pleasure of meeting them and it wasn't until speaking to them both that I felt I had found those missing parts of me.

Lisa and I have the most incredible relationship. A few days after my first reaching out message, Lisa and I talked on the phone and Skype. We have never stopped talking since. Ten years on and I have a big sister who is the most caring, nurturing, resilient, trustworthy, loyal, and loving person you could ever know. I am forever grateful I messaged them that day.

Lisa and her husband came to visit us here in Australia for three weeks and we had the time of our lives. I have also gone to England twice since knowing them. Having the three of us sisters together is one of the most favourite memories of my life. When my first daughter was born, Lisa came out again to Australia to be with us. She was wonderful support for Brendon and I, being there for us as new parents and in awe of her niece.

Here is the thing – it never occurred to me that they couldn't find me. You see my dad adopted me as his own and my name was changed from Lauren Lett to Lauren Harding. My sisters didn't know my name to search for me. I just didn't ever think about that. Perhaps because I was able to learn about my other siblings due to certain family connections I had.

It was always up to me.

All of the thinking and agonising I had about them contacting me if they wanted to when it could only have ever been up to me.

The understanding of mindset, knowing our values, S.E.A.ing our emotions, thinking about what we want to contribute to this world, means actually very little if we don't take action. It is essential to create the behaviours in our daily lives which support and are in alignment to these.

Our relationship to our behaviours - how can we make better decisions in knowing what behaviours are best to start, continue or stop?

Since self-love is all about discernment (which we went through in Chapter Four), let's go through an easy model which allows us to know what the most self-loving thing to do is when it comes to the daily actions we take and the habits we create for ourselves.

I'd like to share a model with you I came across in the coaching industry. I love it as a way for us to continuously check in and evaluate our behaviours with where we spend our time and energy. This model can be described as "The 4 Levels of Experience."

The 4 Levels of Experience

Let's begin at understanding Level 4 and work our way upwards to Level 1 since Level 4 is the least desirable place to be and where our non-self-loving behaviours start. We want to work towards having as many of our behaviours in the Level 1 category as possible.

Level 4:
    Do what does **not** feel good
    Is not good for me and not fulfilling my potential
    Is not good for others
    Is not good for the greater good
    Examples of behaviours in this level include:

- Addictions that no longer even feel good to the person (this is Level 3 behaviour moving down into Level 4) since what started as a way of temporarily feeling good has now become so self-destructive at this bottom level.

    These are any types of addictions such as scrolling social media to the point you don't even enjoy it anymore yet do it out of habit. Watching too much TV or any other type of attachment to external stimuli like drugs, alcohol, smoking, sugar, sex, food, and so on.
- Staying in Level 3 behaviours for too long, which means staying inside our comfort zones, allows behaviours that felt good but were not good for self or anyone else to develop into larger concerns like depression, burn out and living without any purpose or passion. We then slide down into Level 4 behaviours.

Do you have any behaviours in Level 4 and are you ready to let go of them?

Level 3:
Do what feels good
Is not good for me or not fulfilling my potential
Is not good for others
Is not good for the greater good
Examples of behaviours in this level include:

- Procrastination is a great example of being in Level 3. When we have something we know is important to us, we want to do it and yet find ourselves doing everything else but the one thing we want to be doing, chances are this is because the thing is not in our comfort zone. We don't yet have a strategy (step by step process) for it, so instead we default to known and comfortable behaviours which feel good to us, but they don't serve anyone else or fulfil our potential.

- Self-care activities where we enjoy filling up on our own pleasure, enjoyment and self-love buckets are generally in Level 3. Watching TV and eating chocolate is of no service to anyone else unless we are filling up our self-care bucket to then move up to Level 2 and 1 behaviours. It takes a lot of self-awareness and honesty with ourselves to know if doing things for self that feel good are in balance and ultimately encourage, motivate and energise us to move up levels for our contribution to take place.

Do you have any behaviours in Level 3 which are not filling you up, but rather are just your default positions of certainty and habit?

If so, are you ready to let go of them? Do you have resourceful ways to fill up your buckets of self-care and enjoyment which allow you to have more energy for helping others and fulfilling your potential?

Special Note: "The greater good" can be as micro or macro as makes sense to you. For example, "the greater good" could mean your immediate family to start with. Since there is the ripple effect of what is good for a family can then flow out into what is best for the people and places that family are surrounded by. For all our actions, we can have a bigger picture in mind of what is best for the people surrounding this family, all the way out to the local town, the state you live in, the entire community and out to all of humanity. For example, recycling in the family home and other decisions can be for the greater good of humanity relating to climate change. Small changes at a personal level can create big results and ripple effects.

Level 2:
    Do what does **not** feel good
    Is good for me
    Is good for others
    Is good for the greater good
    Examples of behaviours in this level include:

- Doing things outside of our comfort zone which at first don't feel good to us but are best for us. Due to going outside of our comfort zone to fulfil more of our potential, it serves the greater good too. This could be learning a new skill, perhaps doing something for the first time which is part of your contribution in helping others.
- This could be writing that book, learning more efficient ways to run our household, or organising our lives. It's not fun to start with yet these are those crucial life tasks which improve our lives long term.

This level is a good place to go back to your life values you elicited from Chapter Three and see where more alignment to them could happen. For example, if health is important to you, do you need to improve your diet and exercise practices?

At this level, things will feel uncomfortable at first and are likely to bring up self-doubt, critical self-talk and negative emotions. This is your mind thinking it is protecting your old self with what they know. Anything new can threaten the body and mind. Observing the thoughts and feelings by SEAing your emotions, will eventually lead you into level 1 behaviours. These new behaviours will become your new normal and identity.

Are there things you are not doing that you know you need to do?

Level 1:
   Do what feels good
   Is good for me
   Is good for others
   Is good for the greater good
   Examples of behaviours in this level include:

- ♥ This is the level where what used to be out of our comfort zone is now part of who we are since we have mastered the skills, growth and learning, to a point where we do these behaviours easily and automatically.

This could be mastering our health practices which are now just part of our daily lives. Running our household in a newly efficient way, and communicating at a deeper level of connection, and so on.

I believe it is at this level and in Level 2 where we come back home to ourselves. Another way to explain this is by asking ourselves; is the behaviour I am currently doing adding to the light or not? The light being the brightest, purest, most resourcefully expressed version of your potential – do you feel closer to your soul/spirit or not? If we are not bringing more light to our world, are we bringing in more shadow/struggle/chaos?

Let us constantly be asking ourselves;

- ♥ Can I do this better?
- ♥ Am I in alignment with who I want to be?
- ♥ Am I contributing my light and authentic self to the world?
- ♥ Is this behaviour really something I want to fill up my life with? Am I truly enjoying spending time and energy on this?

How do we make long-lasting, deep, and profound change to improve our lives?

How do we make long-lasting, deep and profound change? The simple answer is by making changes in any of our filters, shown with the NLP Communication Model. These filters again consist of changing our perceptions of memories by clearing negative influences, emotions and beliefs we picked up from past events. Also, when changing our values and beliefs, consideration must be given to how we use language toward ourselves and others and even how we process information, such as practising thinking in more detail if we are generally big picture thinkers, etc. (we call this our Meta Programs).

The best place to start changing and improving our lives is by first resolving influences, emotions, and beliefs. Usually, all of the rest of the filters then change organically as a result of our processing. We use Matrix Therapies® to resolve many layers of negative emotions and limiting beliefs in a short period of time. It is a beautifully relaxing and cleansing process of, closing your eyes, being guided to use your imagination to connect with your body and mind. If you would like more information about Matrix Therapies®, please be in touch with me.

There is another model in NLP inspired by anthropologist Gregory Bateson and created by Robert Dilts. It is called the Neurological Levels. I have come across this model in my own study since it wasn't something directly taught to me in my NLP Training. Think of a triangle with 5 levels where the word *Identity* sits at the pointer top of it, underneath that there is a level of *Values and Beliefs*, then *Capabilities*, then *Behaviour* and at the bottom, *Environment*. Above the triangle, beyond it all is *Purpose*.

The model of Neurological Levels is a useful snapshot of how each part of these aspects and levels affects each other and influences the level above and below. Since we want to change our behaviours into Level 1 behaviours as much as possible, we can only do this by considering making a change in all of the other levels, too. Such as changing our environment, our beliefs, values, and identity.

Environment refers to anything outside you, including people, places, things and even the energy around you. Does your environment bring peace and calm, or does it overwhelm you and feel chaotic? Our environment plays a big role in our behaviour.

Behaviour refers to what you say and do. Our behaviour is the surface level of what we see, hear, feel and do, which sits in our environment, and all the other aspects including our capabilities, our beliefs and values.

Capabilities refer to how we do what we do. They are our competencies and skills according to our unique talents. This relates here because we need to consider how we can change behaviours in a way where we have the knowledge and skills to do so.

Values and beliefs are what we covered in Chapter Three, as the things we prioritise that are important to us. Also, the surrounding beliefs we have about our values. Such as, if health is a value of ours, we have certain beliefs about what it means to be healthy.

Identity means how we think about ourselves. If someone asked you, 'Who are you?' what would you answer? Possible answers could range from a wife, a mother, a good person, a human being, a spirit in a human body, an optimist, or an answer related to your work. Any label we put to our self-identity shows our thinking when answering the question.

Lastly, **purpose** refers to what we covered in Chapter Seven with any belief we have beyond self. It might include any bigger visions we have for our lives and the bigger picture that we belong to, such as our faith, feeling a part of a community, our mission in life, or whatever it is for you.

Our thinking about ourselves at the higher levels (purpose and identity) will determine our thinking and behaviour at the lower levels. It's much easier to change our behaviours when we have changed our priority (value) because we have decided to make it more important (a change in belief) than trying to change behaviour with willpower. Willpower comes with old beliefs, values and perceptions of self that are still limiting, so we must consider making a change at a higher level of purpose and identity.

For the above reason, I encourage us to implement each chapter topic to work on our purpose, which affects our identity. Our identity with how we see ourselves will influence changing our values and beliefs, giving us focus on enhancing our skills and capabilities on the right things. Then our new behaviours will become a part of our new self, and our environment will change organically.

Read that again. It summarises the way we improve our lives.

It is also helpful to look at making a change in a lower level (environment, behaviour, capabilities) to help us make a change in the short term. An example of a short-term change that could ripple out to support the higher levels is to change your environment. There are many mindset courses I have done, say on money mindset, for example, where the trainer has said the first thing to do is to declutter anything you no longer use or love. Seemingly unrelated to money, yet the impact of changing our environment can make a significant impact on how we feel. This affects our thoughts, affecting our beliefs, and before we know it, we are behaving differently.

It would be much easier to start eating healthy if you had the right foods in your environment, for instance. It's then crucial to make a change in our priorities with our health, or we will only default back to old beliefs, values, and self-perception (identity). In this example, what if we were to change our iden-tity to someone who puts health above everything else? The new identity could be – 'I am a healthy person, and I value my health over all else. I believe if I put my health first, I can serve my family better and contribute my purpose to a higher level.' When someone works on this being their absolute truth, things like eating well become a part of who they are and therefore a natural, normal behaviour. It is important to consider our capabilities because we can only know the appropriate action when we have the information and knowledge. For example, the knowledge to know what is best for our health so we know what action to take.

When I think of this model, too, and these levels, I change up the order a little bit by starting up the top with identity, jumping to the bottom with environment and then including some of the smaller but significant things we do internally, and it looks like this cycle:

Example of the above:

- ♥ Identity & Values: I am an organised person who values ease and beauty.
- ♥ Environment & Capabilities: Organises outside environment of home, car, office and only has loved and beautiful items. Learns new ways to be organised and asks for support if necessary to learn.
- ♥ Stories (self-talk): I love how my organisation helps me create balance and ease in my life.
- ♥ Beliefs: The more I create ways to be organised, the more

ease I create. I believe I can be well organised. I love being organised.
- ♥ Emotions: I feel so proud of my organisation and feel excited about how much easier my life is becoming.
- ♥ Behaviours: Creates more and more ways to be organised.

Back to:

- ♥ Identity & Values: I am an efficient person who can keep up with life because I have created ways I can do more of what is most important to me.
- ♥ Environment & Capabilities: Continuously growing in the way of organising life. I declutter and look after what I have.
- ♥ Stories (self-talk): I don't have to be perfect, I am just in process of finding more and more ways to create ease and focus on the most important things to me.
- ♥ Beliefs: I am living my life aligned with my highest priorities.
- ♥ Emotions: I am so proud of myself for finding ways to improve my life. I feel happy with how beautiful and more at ease my life feels.
- ♥ Behaviours: Finding creative ways to have rituals and routines to love myself enough to live according to my highest values.

Therefore, this cycle of improvement goes on and on.

Self-loving resources to make the most of our external environment

When it comes to implementing the teachings of the chapters of this book into our daily lives, I have summarised the resources for all the possible ways we can take advantage of our inner and outer worlds.

At the end of each chapter, I have shared how we can apply these resources to self-love and how they are the bridge from just reading the theory to manifesting the results we want in our lives. You will see now as you go back and look in the section "Devoting yourself to applying the learnings in this chapter" it will mention a few of the eight possible resources explained below.

These resources are:

1) Mindset:
This could be a mindset or emotional block stopping us from receiving what we need to make a change in.

Mindset also includes any inner resourcefulness we need to tap into, such as courage, confidence, focus, clarity, inspiration, vulnerability, discernment, love, and so on.

A way to discover our mindset is by writing our thoughts down to discover a possible limiting belief and uncover where it came from. Journaling or talking it through with someone is a way for us to discover a mindset block.

Mindset also includes getting conscious of our purpose, identity, values, and beliefs. Anything that is unseen (the feminine side of us) and becoming aware of these (our masculine side of us) connects to conceiving a new version of ourselves, a higher level of fulfilling our potential.

At the end of each chapter, I have forgiveness as a stand-alone resource because it is so important for self-love.

2) Intuition:
This is our wise, calm inner voice. It is our gut and body wisdom, our inner mentor to trust and follow. We all need to learn how to listen to our intuition more often and deepen our relationship with this inner wise one. Our intuition is our most profound and most trustworthy resource. We spoke about how to connect with it in Chapter Seven.

3) Support:
We may need more support on a particular issue to take action on the right thing for ourselves. Depending on the area of life we focus on, support sources can range from a book, a course, a friend, a teacher, a coach, a cleaner, a cook - the list can go on. We could call upon so much more support when we have enough self-love to do so. This resource can help us by tapping into our ability to ask for and receive the help we need. It is also the ability to recognise we need further support and to be vulnerable enough to find ways to ask for it and benefit from it.

3a) Supportive Environment:
This includes the material world around us and how it either supports us in how we organise it, how it makes us feel if it inspires us or not, and everything the external world could encompass for us. Such as housing, material possessions, access to fresh air and our basic needs. It

includes all places like our home, car, office, our neighbourhood location, and community.

3b) Support from Others:
Do you have people there to listen to you and help you in ways you need? How do you feel about asking others for help? Asking for help is such a self-loving thing to do. Having the right people in your life is also about your ability to nurture relationships, discern people wisely, and communicate effectively.

4) Creativity:
Our ability to solve problems with our creativity and imagination is a powerful resource to remember. The act of journaling is our creativity allowing our thoughts to flow through us and onto paper.

Another way is to view any problem from a different perspective. In doing so, we are using our imagination to come up with another angle to solve it.

5) Structure:
This is about how we organise ourselves, so it can include a ritual, a habit, a routine, a practice, or any structure which allows us to create our new desired behaviours, in order for them to become natural and easy. How can we create ways for our desired behaviours to become so much a part of our daily lives that they are automatic to us and become part of who we are? Is it using a planner, a journal, or a particular app on our phone or computer? Is it a timetable to stick to? Is it doing some exciting goal setting and then creating a way to check

in with your progression towards your goals regularly? There are infinite possibilities to create ways to be organised that work for your unique energy and what inspires you.

6) Tools:
A tool is an external resource that could make all the difference between something being easy for us or not. For instance, in line with the previous examples I have mentioned, a journal and a great pen are excellent tools. It's incredible how we all have many tools to take advantage of. An example of how this resource can help us implement a key to self-love is: to ask ourselves if the tool we are using, like our mobile phone, is helping us to live more of our potential, increase efficiency and ease? Or if it does not? Ask yourself: What tool can help me do this more efficiently and make my life easier? Just like support, our ability to receive support in terms of a tool can ease our lives.

A free tool I have created for you is my self-love planner. It is a three-month planner that has space to create vision boards for your ideal life for three years, twelve months and three months out from today. It has a weekly and daily planner with daily self-love questions and a place for your gratitude. You can access your copy at www.laurenjobson.com/bookfreecourse

7) Action:
Notice all of these resources above assume some form of action.

These resources should all lead to health. We can only do something successfully or easily with the foundation of physical health.

To summarise the above and introduce the concept of health, let's look at it this way:

8) Health

1. We need to have a healthy mindset. This includes forgiveness. To forgive ourselves and others is to clear the mind and be at peace. It is also healthy for the body to release any tight and toxic energy we hold on to if we don't forgive. I have categorised forgiveness with mindset because I do think it is a mental process to undertake with our body and our hearts.
2. We need to have a healthy relationship with our body and our inner voice to be able to listen to our intuition. When we are connected with our bodies, we can notice it's signals to tell us what is best for us and what is not.
3. When it comes to support, we need to make sure our physical bodies are supported to be healthy on all levels, physically, mentally, emotionally, and spiritually. What support from others do you need to help you improve your physical health? How can you set up your environment to support your health?
4. Our connection to creativity needs us to use our imagination in healthy ways. Create ways to do exercise for example, that inspire you and that you can maintain.
5. We can have structures which allow us to look after our physical health. What routines do you need to set up to take action with your health?
6. We can take advantage of tools which allow us to look after our physical health. Is it a home gym? Is it a tool for the kitchen to help make easy healthy meals?
7. We need to continually take action towards better physical health.

Creating motivation

In NLP, we study what steps people take both inside their mind and in actions externally that create excellent results. How do we create motivation towards our goals? One last time, I refer to part of the NLP Communication Model.

Internal Representation from the NLP Communication Model

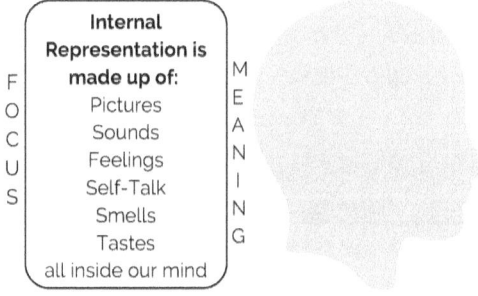

What you see above is extremely powerful to know. It is perhaps one of my favourite things about NLP. Our internal representation (IR) describes how we create meaning to everything in our lives. Our meaning shows us what we focus on and most importantly, determines our behaviours. Our IR is created once an external event has been processed through our five senses and our unconscious filters. It is simply the pictures (and movies), sounds, feelings, self-talk, smells and tastes we have in our conscious awareness at any time. Our awareness is so fleeting in each moment, a lot of the time we don't even pay attention to these things we have in our mind.

Here is an example of our IR at play. I want you to think of your favourite holiday destination. It can be somewhere you have been before or somewhere new you would like to go. As you think about going on holidays here, notice now what you are picturing in your mind. Are you in the picture or are you looking through your own eyes? Are there any sounds that are important? How do you feel in your body when you think of this? What is your self-talk? Can you smell and taste anything as you think of this holiday? Hmm I can taste a nice cold drink and smell sea water. This is your internal representation. I hope that was a fun IR to connect with and it has a positive meaning for you.

We have internal representations for anything we can think about. This is our meaning making machine. Our filters again, determine how we create meaning and yet, we can make a change with our IR to affect our behaviours, sometimes without having to change a filter. For instance, I want you to think about making money. How you think about making money is created by your money beliefs, memories you have with money, how you value it, the influences you have had around money and so on. If you would like to change your relationship to how you make money, changing your filter is going to make the most profound and lasting change. Many things mentioned in this book explain how we can make change here at the unconscious level. And, we can play with our IR now to possibly make a change too. I want you to think about making money. And I want you to change your IR to a movie of you having so much money you are rolling in cash, happy. See – see how quickly you can change a thought! We can play with the movies, feelings and self-talk in our mind in one moment.

To find motivation to take more action, again, make change

inside a filter (values, beliefs etc) and you can also picture the thing you want more motivation to do, in your mind. Then all you need to do is imagine yourself doing the behaviour successfully. It can feel really inspiring to look through your own eyes as if you are already doing it now. But – and I always use the word 'but' intentionally, make sure you also see your body doing the behaviour too, not just through your own eyes. The movie is of you doing the behaviour and to the successful completion of it. This is like you were watching a video of you doing it on your phone. Notice all the good feelings you will have when it is done. Make the colours of this movie, bright in your mind. Any positive sensations in your body, make stronger and more compelling. Add any sound that could be important and exciting to you, perhaps receiving compliments from others, a clapping audience or your favourite song playing - whatever is most appropriate and motivating to you. Finally, make sure your self-talk is positive and powerful. What are you saying to yourself when you are successfully doing and completing this behaviour?

Have a play with how you think of things inside your mind and notice how your body reacts and your motivation to start, increases. Now go do the thing! What thing? – It is time to set some goals!

Setting goals for the life we want to experience and from knowing we love ourselves enough to create it

Setting goals in each area of our lives lets us know what

path we intend to embark on. If we don't set intentions and goals for who we want to be, what we want to experience and achieve, who we want to have in our lives and more, we let time fly by without knowing how we have spent it. There will be times in our lives when we narrow our focus to what is most important to us. Such as raising children, looking after elderly parents, recovering from an illness or injury and hence, our goals in other areas become less important. It is in times like these where I think we simply acknowledge our intentions to be present and to show up in the way we want to. This is a version of a goal too.

From all the work I have done in NLP with how focussed it is on achieving what we want, my favourite way to goal set is by imagining who we want to be in three years' time from now. I love the number three because this amount of time goes by quick enough to feel we can set some realistic and exciting goals while having a fair idea of where we might be and how our life looks. Yet is not too close to today either so we can set some big, audacious, beautiful goals which can feel a great stretch from what we have and who we are now.

We have so many areas of life to consider when thinking about what we want to achieve. By understanding how our brain can only cope with up to nine chunks of information at a time, I love to mind map my goals first. What do I mean by this? Well, to grab a big piece of paper and to map out those bigger chunks of our lives we want to prioritise and set goals in. We call these "areas of life". I have some ideas for the different areas of life below.

Possible areas of life. You can create your own labels, such as 'work' instead of 'contribution'.

For example, over the next three years you may want to work on your home improvements, family time with holidays together, health, financial growth and feeling more inspired through your spiritual connection and contribution. What I encourage is to write these down as the bigger categories to focus on. Then from these you can write more detail for each area. This is mind mapping. I have a video of me showing you how to do this with the free access to my self-love planner. The planner has a space to mind map your goals and more. As mentioned, It is a three-month planner that has space to create vision boards for your ideal life for three years, twelve months and three months out from today. It has a weekly and daily planner with daily self-love questions and a place for your gratitude. You can access your copy at www.laurenjobson.com/bookfreecourse

As you will see in the planner too, it shows you how I encourage us to write out our goals which considers all the important factors when it comes to goal setting. To write a powerful goal we can state it like it has already happened. See the example below:

It is now March 2026; I am 39 years old and turning 40 later this year. I am so grateful my family is healthy and we are excited for our overseas trip to England for their summer this year. In the last three years...

I have achieved this...

I feel this...

I am so grateful we can do this...

Can you see how fun it can be to write out and think about your goals? I love how when I start to write them like this, with stating your age too as it's a great measurement of time, you can free flow into what your imagination brings up for you. This process shows you what you want before you have even thought about it. It turns out I want to go to England to see my sister Lisa in three years, that's exciting!

Before you head over to access your self-love planner if you haven't already, I also want to mention how profound and fun it is to set goals from our Passion and Purpose Archetypes when we know these about ourselves. I can connect with what The Lovers, The Innocent Adventurer, The Creative Nurturer and The Knight wants for me because these are the best and most passionate parts of me. Setting goals from them is incredibly aligned with my highest potential and what I want for my best most self-loving life. If you don't know yours, you can also go back to your values you discovered from Chapter Three and make sure your values are incorporated into your goals.

Conclusion of this vow

I vow to take action with supportive and intentional behaviours.
I honour the relationship I have with my external world and how I show up in it.

I'd love for you to consider that by reading this book and taking action on all of my recommended activities, you can embrace your best self and take the most self-loving action. Revise your daily habits to notice if they are in Level 1 and 2 behaviours and Level 3 for filling up your self-care buckets. This is not about thinking that we need to create perfect lives; because life is for living, learning, going off track only to have ways to come back on track. The resources I mention in this book are here to return home to yourself when life has taken you off your path. We leave home, we come back home. Go gentle and easy on your judgements too, remember.

Finally, be sure to write out your goals with a pen and a planner/journal/big piece of paper that inspires you. Having your desires, dreams, imagination, and future visions of yourself flowing from your mind and body, down your arm and through your hand is a powerful way to ask for what you want. I have created a guided process to take you out into your ideal future to help you connect to your goals if you need some extra support with this.

A summary of what you learned in
Chapter Nine

I vow to take action with supportive and intentional behaviours.

I honour the relationship I have with my external world and how I show up in it.

- Lauren's story about connecting with her sisters
- Our relationship to our behaviours - how can we make better decisions in knowing what behaviours are best to start, continue or stop?
- The 4 Levels of Experience
- How do we make long-lasting, deep, and profound changes to improve our lives?
- Self-loving resources to make the most of our external environment
- Creating motivation
- Setting goals for the life we want to experience and from knowing we love ourselves enough to create it

Devoting yourself to applying the learnings in this chapter:

1. Using the Self-Loving Resource of Tools: Grab your journal or my workbook I created for you at www.laurenjobson.com/bookfreecourse

Answer the questions about what behaviours you may have for each of the levels of experience. You could write down an entire list of all the behaviours you fill up your days with. Then, notice which ones are serving you since they are good for you, good for others and good for the greater good. Notice which behaviours need to be changed, improved or let go of. Notice and commit to new behaviours which will fulfill a desired version of yourself.

2. Using the Self-Loving Resource of Support: A Matrix Therapies® and NLP Master Practitioner can help you remove any blocks such as limiting beliefs and emotions you might have become aware of from this chapter and the exercise above.

Also, the support from your external environment is important here. Look around for what you have in your environments which include your home, office, car and anything you carry around with you on a daily basis. Your environment is here to support your life, not the other way around. Create your external world to help you have ease in setting up new behaviours. You're not going to do the exercise if your gym gear is hidden away or you don't have what you need to get started. Declutter the things that are making life hard and invite supportive tools and resources to make things easier.

3. Using the Self-Loving Resource of Action: All of this information in this chapter could just be interesting theory until we devote ourselves to taking applied action. Answer the questions from this chapter and be sure to grab your journal and use the tool of my online course.

My final thoughts on Self-Love to you, my beloved reader

We don't need to change. Not really. We need to love and accept ourselves as we are today. If we did, we would become even more loving to others as a result too.

In the process of loving and accepting who we are today, naturally, the limiting beliefs we have about ourselves will want to fall away. If we can love and accept ourselves with the problems we have now, we can love ourselves without them too. When we love and accept ourselves as we are today, we can naturally change our values to prioritise things we haven't made important in the past. We would put ourselves up higher on the importance list. We would have our health higher up in the importance list. We would communicate both to ourselves and others more lovingly and effectively.

This book is not about changing yourself. It is about being more of who you are.

It is about cutting away all the outside negative influences that are not you.

Whenever I have mentioned giving birth to a new you, or fulfilling a better version of yourself, it's still you. You are perfectly human as you are today. And you will remain perfectly human tomorrow.

I hope this book has given you new ideas and strategies to

improve your life and the way you feel about yourself.

Remember, your happily ever after is not about being happy all the time because that's simply not the plan of human experience. Your happily ever after is knowing your way back home to your beautiful self.

I encourage you to pick up this book time and time again to review, plan, and act to make changes in your life to bring more love, lightness, joy, purpose and self-love to it.

You are your only home. You might as well enjoy it! You are worthy, you are good enough and free to love life. Go and be more of you – life will love you back for it.

A note from my grandmothers on self-love

Since I have the blessing of having both my grandmothers with us, I asked them for their advice by asking: 'If you could give one piece of advice to Amber, Hazel and Aurora (their great-granddaughters) about the relationship they have with themselves, from what you have learned through your own life, what would it be?'

My Abuela replied: 'To be kind and have respect for yourself and towards others, in the hope that it will be reciprocated.'

My Nan replied: 'Go and try everything you feel you want to do. If you don't want to do something, that's fine. If you want to do something, let go of your fear and give it a go. To have no regrets and to know you went for what you wanted, you can be proud of that. Enjoy life. There is so much to offer and when you see an opportunity, jump in.'

My main influences and appreciation

I have been hugely influenced, of course, from all the things I have learned from being in the personal development field of Neuro Linguistic Programming (NLP), since 2004. It is a big contributor to what I share here throughout the chap-ters. I thank my Uncle Simon, for introducing me to Personal Development through my experience with my therapist but also his passion for it and allowing me to pick up many amazing books from his shelf from a young age. Thank you for believing in me Simon, then and now. You directly started me on the path to my genius in NLP and beyond this have always been a beacon of support and inspiration to me. I love you.

One of my biggest contributors to my knowledge and what has allowed me to find my own expression of the wisdom of the Source, to which we are all connected, is the true genius of who I can gratefully say is a dear friend of mine, Pip McKay.

Pip McKay is a Pioneer in the field of Personal Development, who created Matrix Therapies® and Archetypal Coaching®. I have the true privilege and honour to be able to teach her work which she has created from her genius. You will notice I have mentioned her at least a few times in this book. My deepest and immense gratitude and adoration goes out to her from me. Thank you, Pip. I love you.

Lauren's gratitude

As I mentioned at the start of the book, my gratitude for my husband is immense. I need to mention him again here because this mammoth achievement of writing this book is most directly attributed to who he is as a supporter of me. I think he must be utterly tired of hearing about how I need to go and work on my book. It has taken me three years of officially starting and completing this. There are washing baskets of clean clothing sprawled throughout the house, living out of them because any chance I had between breastfeeding and all the other needs of our 6-month-old plus helping our five-year-old transition to big school, I go into my office to write and complete this. It's the 14th of February 2023 and I am crying with gratitude that this final manuscript is being sent to my typesetter (interior book designer) today. The work continues and he never complains of the evenings I spend in here. I love you immensely my love. I see you and I know I am the luckiest. You are our superhero, always. Thank you.

To Mum and Dad, thank you so much for being the most incredible parents. There are so many times I now look back and think – oh my goodness, my parents did so much for me and did so well – now that I have the privilege and challenge of being a parent myself. Thank you for supporting me. Thank you for giving me every chance and opportunity to be happy and healthy. I love you Mum and Dad, so much.

Thank you to Fran and Jono for being the best siblings I could have ever grown up with. You both know there is nothing half about you. We have always grown up never thinking about how we were created a little differently. It's a true pleasure and honour to be your big sister and to annoy you and all that comes with it. I remember your birthdays so clearly and knew then what I know now - my whole world has just changed for the better, someone incredible has come into my life! I love you both so much!

Thank you, Meg, for being my sister and best friend since we were both six years old. You said it so beautifully recently and I wish I had said it first myself – I wouldn't be me if I didn't have you. I am so grateful we have the memories we do together. They are so deeply special and are always ours. I am so grateful to share life with you to create many more amazing memories together and am ever so lucky for your unwavering support. I love you. You inspire me more than you know.

Thank you, Lisa, for coming back into my life. You are the sister everyone needs and we're the luckiest to have you in our lives. I could never have imagined in my wildest and most ideal dreams how amazing you could be and how much richer my life has become since you have been in it (again). You are one of the most incredible humans I know from your resilience, your strength of character and love you give. You remind all those who know you how to just be a good person. Fran, Jono, and I now have you as a big sister and we love you loads. Now get your butt over to Australia again please and thank you.

Thank you to Felicity, John, Lynette, Anthony, Jaymie, and Mikey. I feel so blessed to have the most incredible in-laws anyone could ever ask for. To have love in my life and be rewarded with having you in my life too, as an extension from that love is really special. Felicity, you truly are the most wonderful mother in love anyone could ever have! Thank you for everything you do for us and for being beautiful you. We love you.

Thank you to my Aunt Annie, my Nan and Abuela. To both of my Grandads. I love you all so much!

Thank you Louise for coming back into my life. You are a beautiful person.

To my soul sisters who would take up another hundred pages if I listed why I loved you all. Thank you to Shona for all the years of support in my business with the time, patience, skills and beauty you have given to me. Thank you mostly though for our friendship. Thank you, Jess Mooney for your support, love, patience, and reminder to me to enjoy life. Thank you to Sonya and Jess for being you. Becoming Trainers too of teaching this magic, is so inspirational to me and all credit to you for the work you have done to make it happen. You both are incredible humans, and I am so grateful for your continued support, wisdom and love! I have so much love for you both. Thank you, Jess Lowe, for coming into my life via Instagram. You are a beautiful friend and human being! Thank you to amazing Karen for your incredible generosity of time and love over the many years. To grow together and to think how far we have come – wow! To darling Steph, our friendship has lasted miles and milestones, I am so grateful we have kept in touch and for our deep conversations and love you share with me. I love you.

To those who have crossed my path in my career and become my darling friends; Mark Bowness, Leila Lutz, Andrew Low, Cathy Valentine, Amy McCann, Jan Cobb, Janet Beaud, Candy Wright, Roslyn Vecellio, Fiona Brown, Theresa Lynch, Ainslie Graham, Amie Lyttle, Catherine Bell, Ann Wood, Heidi Heron, Antoniette Gomez, Cassandra Webb, Brianna Squires, Kelley Wacher, Christina Loizou, Daniel Davison, Dee Jay and Jo Jo Jackson, Suzie, Deborah Edwards, Fiona Davidson, Krystyna Andreoni, Kylie Ryan, Will Hickey, Lynda Holt, Mei Ouw, Nadine Bowen, Rebecca Newman, – thank you for being in my life and being you.

Thank you to Mia Sipidias, Carmel May, Anthony Ferro, Kylie Clift, James Thomas, Anna Grindley and Tracey Gillies for your support, friendship and guidance over the years.

A big and special thank you to Emma Franklin-Bell for being my book writing coach. I remember where I was when I knew I would have my book out there in the world because of your support. I received an email from you after our connection we made and here I am, finishing this book, a big reason is because of you. You are wonderful in so many ways. Thank you for helping me manifest this dream of mine – it's been a gift of self-belief at a whole new level.

Thank you to Zahrina Robertson, Karen Crombie, Dania Zafar and Emma Bennetts for your contribution to this book with photos, editing, typesetting and cover design.

Please forgive me if you know I love you and I haven't mentioned your name here. I do love and appreciate you. Thank you to all those mentioned in the book who will remain anonymous.

And to my greatest teachers, biggest blessings, and main inspiration to complete this book – thank you to my daughters. Darling Amber for teaching me how strong I am and for truly inspiring me to be a better human every single day.

Darling Aurora for reminding me to enjoy this life and showing me that life can be much easier than I make it sometimes.

Thank you so much for reading this book! I truly hope it has touched your heart and inspired you to create a better life for yourself in a lot of ways. Thank you for trusting me with your time.

About the Author

Lauren Jobson is an award-winning NLP Master Trainer, internationally certified Matrix Therapies® Master Trainer and Coach. A Master Trainer means she teaches the teachers of the coaches as well as certifying hundreds of coaches all across Australia and now online, globally. Along with other modalities such as Hypnosis, Chakra Mindset, and the Universal Laws through Archetypes.

Since 2009 she has trained NLP and since 2012, Matrix Therapies®.

Certified Matrix Therapies® Master Trainer by the creator of Matrix Therapies®, Pip McKay.

Lauren teaches all levels of Neuro Linguistic Programming (NLP) which includes:

- ♥ NLP Practitioner Certification Training
- ♥ NLP Master Practitioner Certification Training
- ♥ NLP Trainers Training Certification
- ♥ Plus Hypnosis which are all internationally recognised and meet governing board standards.

Lauren also teaches Archetypal Coaching®, which includes:

- ♥ Evolve Now! Level 1A: Passion and Purpose Coaching™

- Evolve Now! Level 1B: Masculine and Feminine Coaching™
- Evolve Now! Level 1C: Matrix Therapies® Coaching
- Archetypal Coaching® Level 2A: Principles of Manifestation and Love Coaching™
- Archetypal Coaching® Level 2B: Principles of Growth and Abundance Coaching™
- Archetypal Coaching® Level 2C: Principles of Transformation and Influence Coaching™

She has taught thousands of wonderful people around Australia, that say she "transcends age with her wisdom & guidance." Lauren was the Vice Chairperson of the Australian Board of NLP now named NLPAA as high standards in the NLP field are important to her. She is also a Registered Trainer Member and Clinical Member at the NLPAA (NLP Association of Australia) and a Full Member and Recognised Training Provider at IICT (International Institute of Complementary Therapists). Her certifying training school is Intuitive Heart Training Academy Pty Ltd. www.intuitivehearttraining.com.au

References

Below is a list of the books, articles, courses and websites I have referred to throughout the book.

Books, Articles and Courses:
From Chapter Two:
- *Spirit Babies, How to Communicate with the Child You're Meant to Have* by Walter Makichen
- *Anatomy of the Spirit*, by Dr Caroline Myss.
- *You Can Change Your Life*, by Louise L. Hay.
- *Barometer of the Soul*, by Annette Noontil.
- *The Seven Chakra Sisters, Make Friends with the Inner Allies Who Keep You Healthy, Laughing, Loving and Wise*, by Linda Linker Rosenthal

From Chapter Four:
- *The Archetypal Stages of Growth* by Pip McKay taught at Evolve Now! Level 1B: Masculine and Feminine Coaching

From Chapter Five:
- Cognitive Distortions from *Feeling Good: The New Mood Therapy*, by Dr David Burns

From Chapter Seven:
- Dr Karpman, S. B. (1968) The Drama Triangle. *Fairy Tales and Script Drama Analysis*

Websites:

From Chapter Two:
- Sonya Furlong's Music: https://music.youtube.com/watch?v=_qwVmpKWKVY
- Antoniette Gomez *Chakra Mindset Journal and Book*: https://www.amazon.com.au/Antoniette-Gomez/e/B00MJSK01U/ref=dp_byline_cont_book_1

From Chapter Five:
- *The Neuroscience of Self-Compassion* Udemy Course by Kelly McGonigal: https://www.udemy.com/course/kelly-mcgonigal/
- mindmypeelings blog "How Cognitive Distortions Creates an Irrational Perception of Reality" https://www.mindmypeelings.com/blog/cognitive-distortions
- *The Work – Four Questions* by Byron Katie: https://the-work.com/en

From Chapter Six:
- Brené Brown on The Difference Between Guilt and Shame: https://fs.blog/brene-brown-guilt-shame/

From Chapter Nine:
- *Neurological Levels* by Robert Dilts: http://www.nlpu.com/NLPU.html

Connect with the author

To connect with Lauren please email:
lauren@lovelifewithlauren.com.au
Go to: www.laurenjobson.com
Follow on Instagram: @laurenjobson
To get the most out of this book go to:
www.laurenjobson.com/bookfreecourse

Dania Zafar School of Hope

The word placement, spaces, hearts, ease of reading and beauty of this book is Dania's incredible contribution to this book through her incredible genius in typesetting. Sadly, Dania tragically passed away before being able to finish the file, ready to print. With the help of others, through love and appreciation of Dania's work, we made it happen to have her work on these pages.

In memory and in appreciation of Dania's life, Lauren would like to honour her here by sharing how Ignite Publishing Company in Canada have set up the following:

"To honour the genuine and kind soul Dania was and to ensure her legacy of creativity and kindness is remembered forever, Ignite Publishing Company will be building a school in Pakistan, her home country, in her name. The Dania Zafar School of Hope will be a haven for children who dream big and love the arts. They hope this school will provide comfort to Dania's family and create a place for them to honour and celebrate her life."

Lauren is donating a part of the proceeds of this book to the building of this school in Pakistan. She invites you to consider a contribution by going to: www.daniazafarmemorial.com

www.ingramcontent.com/pod-product-compliance
Lightning Source LLC
Chambersburg PA
CBHW030252010526
44107CB00053B/1678